How to Run
a Real Estate Office

How to Run
a Real Estate Office

Dorothy R. Bates, GRI, CRB

Reston Publishing Company, Inc.
A Prentice-Hall Company
Reston, Virginia

Library of Congress Cataloging in Publication Data

Bates, Dorothy R.
    How to run a real estate office.

    Bibliography: p. 215
    Includes index.
    1. Real estate business—Management. 2. Office
management. I. Title.
HD1375.B324   333.33'068   81-15709
ISBN 0-8359-2970-1   AACR2

© 1982 by
Reston Publishing Company, Inc.
A Prentice-Hall Company
Reston, Virginia 22090

10   9   8   7   6   5   4   3

Printed in the United States of America.

Contents

Preface

You are making a decision that can change the rest of your life, whether it's —

- to start running your present office with methods that growing, prospering companies use; or
- to stretch yourself from a career in listing and selling real estate to a career as manager; or
- to go into the real estate business as a brand new entrepreneur.

This book is intended to be a practical working guide for an office manager. While the same basic principles apply to any size office, this is primarily oriented to the manager of a smaller residential real estate office.

This book is about leadership and what it takes to be successful as an entrepreneur. *Funk and Wagnalls International Dictionary* (1978) defines *entrepreneur* as "one who undertakes to start and conduct a business or enterprise, assuming full control and risk".

The basic principles of management apply to every business endeavor. Some businesses are product oriented; some are service oriented. All enterprises involve people. Real estate is service oriented, involving real property and real people.

There is a worldwide trend toward "Bigness". "Big is better", we're told. "Big Government", "Big Business", "Big Brother", etc. There is a time and a place for joining a franchise or a referral service or for adding branch offices, for growth into "Bigness". Can you manage it? Can you retain your identity? Is identity important to you? It's your life — your decision.

Will Rogers said, "If you want to be successful, you gotta know what you are doing, love what you are doing, believe in what you are doing. It's just that simple." While this is basically a primer for those new to a career in real estate office management, old-timers who've been in business 20 years can still learn some more effective business practices and problem-solving techniques.

As I worked on this book over a period of several years, times changed. Laws changed. Besides managing an office, I was giving seminars in office management, listening to the questions of those who attended. What bothered them the most?

Some basic questions remained the same. New questions kept coming up as new laws and new trends affected the industry. Many brokers wanted an easy-out answer. Could they solve all their office problems if they joined a franchise? Or joined a referral service? How could they compete with the giants?

Many resisted the changes taking place in the industry. Some wanted to go back to the "good old days".

There is a definite trend in the real estate field for large corporations and franchises to dominate the industry. I believe there is still room for the old or new smaller company to grow and prosper, despite competition from the corporate giants.

"Small" can be beautiful indeed, when the bottom line shows a healthy profit.

Essential to the success of the small firm are dedication to professional standards, personal service, and diligent follow-up for all sellers and buyers. Management expertise can make a big difference. Knowledge of every law affecting you is vital. Day-to-day control of activities and results is also important. So is the insight to continually study the market, be aware of trends, forecast the future, and guide your company accordingly.

Use this as a workbook to help your firm succeed. Fill out the checklists. Use the style of forms that will be useful, revising them as needed to suit your marketing area. Rewrite the sample letters so that they sound like you; keep them on hand. I realize that this book is not consistent as to gender of brokers or associates, but both men and women have equal opportunity in the real estate field.

James Froude wrote, "Experience teaches slowly, and at the cost of mistakes." Though a lot of lessons have come my way over the years, I wish I'd had an easy-to-follow book like this when I began in 1956. Mistakes could have been avoided, and time and money saved. I love the real estate business and I want to share what I've learned with you.

Dorothy R. Bates

About the Author

Dorothy R. Bates, GRI, CRB, has been a Realtor® since 1956. A graduate of Iowa State University, she was a founding member of the Wilton Board of Realtors and served two years as president. She was a vice-president of the Connecticut Association of Realtors® for three years and in 1971 was chosen Realtor® of the Year by the state. She was a founding member of the Women's Council in Connecticut and served as its state president and governor. She is a member of the Realtors National Marketing Institute® and has served as its membership chairman in Connecticut. In 1974 she achieved the designation of CRB and was a founder and the first president of the New England Chapter of Certified Residential Brokers. She has been Dean of the Graduate Realtors Institute® in Connecticut and is a lecturer on ethics and office management for both Connecticut and Tri-State GRI courses. She was a Chairman of Education for the Connecticut Association of Realtors® and a member of the National Association of Realtors® Committee on Education. She is president of Dorothy R. Bates & Associates, Inc. in Wilton, CT, managing an office with eight associates.

1

Office Management
Basics

Most people choose a real estate career for both profit and pleasure. If there's no profit in the work, you can't afford to stay in the field for long. If there's no pleasure, why choose to continue?

The basic principle for a successful business enterprise is *management by objective*. Specific goals, a written plan to reach them, and a timetable are all essential. It's true that some companies survive without a plan, a structure, or skillful management. It's also probable that about 80 percent of the business in your market area is being achieved by about 20 percent of the competing firms!

To capture a major share of your market potential for listing and sales dollar income, you need proficient management. Skill in planning, executing plans, and measuring results leads to success.

Finally, as a basic principle, your company and its personnel must be service oriented. *You* do not own the properties you have for sale; your clients do. *You* do not own the customer, who may or may not use your services to buy. Your only product is *service*, and the quality of your service influences your success potential.

An old adage, particularly true in our field of real estate, is "Business goes where the service is best." Think for a minute of where you take your car to be serviced, or whom you call when you need household repair work done. If a friend highly recommends someone who rendered superior service, you would take your business there.

1

Policies and Procedures

This dynamic duo implements your basic principles.
They must be:

- Written
- Discussed
- Agreed to by all
- Enforced by management

and reviewed and revised as the times, company structure, and market area change. Awareness of need for change is crucial, whether it stems from a local ordinance or a Supreme Court ruling.

You may hang out your shingle initially as a one-person office. As your business grows you'll need to take on more associates. Your policy and procedure manual will be the company bible. When written, understood, and agreed to, your "P & P" manual will help you save hours of company time, promote fair play, lessen hassles or arguments, and settle disputes. It will also help you achieve team spirit for maximum productivity because all associates play by the same guidelines. Fair is fair, and the company policies and procedures apply to all.

The Manager's Job

With a foundation of sound principles, procedures, and policies, a key ingredient in the success of a company is management.

A one-line job description of a manager might be to attract, train, assist, and retain associates so that individual and company goals are achieved.

This may sound like a simple task. It isn't. And while many listing and selling training aids are available for sales personnel, knowing how to be a manager usually comes from the long, hard school of trial-and-error experience.

Many real estate offices are opened by sales associates who have been highly successful. They have established favorable contacts, sometimes referred to as a "stable". They feel ready to start their own office, but have little management "know how". The star salesperson may turn out to be a third-rate manager.

Ego drive, empathy, energy, and enthusiasm are needed for both jobs—but to different degrees. The high ego drive spurs super sellers on, and they have enough empathy to sense what customers want. Managers get their thrills secondhand, as when an associate makes a big sale. The manager needs less ego drive and more empathy to be perceptive to the needs and wants of all personnel.

Many strong listing and selling associates dislike detail, paperwork, desk work. The manager should be comfortable at a desk, enjoy the necessary recordkeeping, and be attentive to details.

The manager is the team coach, not the superstar. Frequently, the incomes of the top producers will be higher than that of the manager.

Before you move into management, use Table 1-1 to evaluate your strengths and weaknesses.

TABLE 1-1   EVALUATE YOURSELF AS MANAGER

	Yes	No	Could Improve
1. Will you easily attract good sales associates?			
2. Will you have a written training program?			
3. Can you train salespersons to do something which if left to themselves probably wouldn't get done?			
4. Do you consider yourself an assertive person?			
5. Can you make decisions readily?			
6. Do you enjoy problem solving?			
7. Do you know where your firm stands on your board (i.e., #1, #2, or #3) in both listings and sales?			
8. Do you like keeping a budget?			
9. Do you keep good records?			
10. Can you delegate tasks to others?			
11. Are you innovative, willing to try new ideas?			
12. Can you control people without being domineering?			
13. Will you review your P&P manual frequently?			
14. Can you plan regular meetings for your team?			
15. Will you contribute to a favorable office climate?			
16. Do you have good communication skills?			
17. Have you shown leadership ability in community organizations?			
18. Do you have good listening habits?			
19. Is it easy for you to concentrate?			
20. Will you encourage your associates to take courses, join organizations, improve themselves?			
21. Do you manage your time well?			
22. Do you have ways to measure associate effectiveness?			
23. Can you put company goals first (profit) when it means you must fire the bottom producer?			
24. Do you set aside time each week for planning, creating, improving?			

If you can answer "YES" to 18 of these questions, you're on the road to success.

--------------------- *Sales Associates* ---------------------

A brief job description for a sales associate would be as follows: a person with the ability and desire to list and sell enough properties to reach individual and company goals.

Management would also expect cheerful cooperation among all associates, a spirit of teamwork.

Associates expect the following from management:

1. Training in skills to succeed in their job.

2. Opportunity for listing/selling prospects.

3. An attractive, well-run office (which they are proud to be part of).

4. Clearly defined policies and procedures observed by all.

5. Fair treatment of all in office with equal working conditions and benefits for all.

6. Assistance from associates or the manager when sticky problems arise.

7. An adherence by all to the Code of Ethics and professional standards of the National Association of Realtors®.

8. A supply of tools necessary for the job that reflects high company image.

9. Management advertising and promotion of properties.

10. Concern for the associate as a person, with open communication from the manager.

--------------------- *Sellers and Buyers* ---------------------

We now have:

- Basic principles
- The policy and procedures manual
- The manager, using management by objectives
- Sales associates

All we need are *sellers and buyers*. These will be attracted to your company through personal contacts, referrals, and advertising and, when well served, will provide repeat business.

When you have a signed listing on a property, the seller is your *client*. If you distribute the listing through a Multiple Listing Service, any broker who works on the listing is a subagent of the listing broker. Buyers are *prospects* until they own property; then they become potential clients. These relationships may not last unless your firm provides excellent service.

Profit-Oriented Decisions

Profit is not a dirty word. It's the basis of our free enterprise system. The manager's attitude toward profit affects his or her decisions and influences the company's bottom line. But good, sound decisions can be swayed by guilt feelings.

- You determine to add a new associate—you encounter resistance from the present associates.
- You analyze next year's budget and announce a change in commission splits so there will be profit after expenditures—you encounter resentment.

Their resistance and resentment are a challenge. Don't feel guilty. Your associates don't run the office—that's your job. You needn't ride roughshod over their objections to your decisions about company policy, but you can be persuasive and exercise all your communications skills to achieve your objectives.

Damon Runyon said, "The race is not always to the swift, nor the battle to the strong, but that's the way to bet."

Remember that associates are likely to be most concerned about their immediate future—the way things are, what they'll earn this month, this year. The manager looks down the road, next year, five years, and acts accordingly. The manager makes decisions and implements them to achieve the long-term company objectives.

License Laws

Real estate license laws vary from state to state, but the trend is definitely toward increased educational requirements and stiffer examinations. Many states have different requirements for a salesperson's license than for a broker's license. Generally, the broker's license requires more classroom hours, requires passing a more difficult exam, and may require some years of experience as a salesperson to qualify. (See state license regulations in the Appendix.)

Real estate commissions govern the industry within their respective states and establish license laws. Some states have reciprocity whereby licensing in one state enables you to obtain a license in another state by simply completing an application and paying a fee.

Once licensed, a real estate broker must be familiar with all federal and state legislation that affects the industry.

Are you familiar with the federal usury law? Does your state have a usury law in addition?

We live in a sea of initials: CZM, EPA, FH, FTC, HUD, IRS, MMW, NCA, OILSR, SEC, UGNCD*, for example.

We live in a jungle of jargon: Fannie Mae, Ginnie Mae, balloons, wraparounds, V.M.I., and M.I.D., refer to some of the ways to finance real property. An F.S.B.O. is a "fizzbo" or "For Sale By Owner".

In our industry, words and phrases vary from state to state and from area to area. Conveyance of title is called a *closing* in Connecticut. It's called a *passing* in Massachusetts. Perhaps you call it a *settlement* or use some other word.

Some states require ongoing education to renew a license, a trend likely to be more widespread.

You can obtain current license law information for your state by writing to the real estate commission at your state capital building.

Board of Realtors®

Those licensees who join their local board of Realtors® must abide by the Code of Ethics of the National Association of Realtors®. Because the code is updated from time to time, it should be reviewed annually by all members.

What are the advantages of joining your local board of Realtors®, plus your state association and the National Association of Realtors®? It distinguishes those who have chosen real estate as a career from those who like to have a license "just in case" they have a chance to list or sell a property or those who simply prefer to be independent brokers. Your professional organizations provide you with many advantages including current information on the real estate market, economic factors and legislation affecting the business, and educational opportunities.

Being a member of the Multiple Listing Service in your marketing area provides you with a simple method for sharing your listings with other brokers. It provides your clients with greater marketing exposure of their property. It enables your office to show prospects a wide choice of properties, not just your own listings.

---

*Coastal Zone Management, Environmental Protection Agency, Fair Housing, Federal Trade Commission, Housing and Urban Development, Internal Revenue Service, Magnuson–Moss Warranty Act, New Communities Act, Office of Interstate Land Sales Registration, Securities and Exchange Commission, Urban Growth and New Community Development Act.

_____ *Continuing Education* _____

Do you know what the following designations mean: GRI, CRS, CRB, CCIM, MAI, RM, CPM, CRE?*

What designations will be of value to you and your associates? What are the educational and other requirements to achieve these designations? They signify expertise in a chosen field, although their use is relatively new in the real estate industry. There was a time when CPA was a new set of initials in business. Today most of us know the difference between a book-keeper and a Certified Public Accountant. Public awareness of expertise is growing in our career field of real estate, too.

The courses required to achieve a designation from the Realtors National Marketing Institute® are a challenge, but if a manager stops learning, he or she will soon be out of step with the times.

Many other educational opportunities are available to a manager keenly interested in acquiring more knowledge and skill: conventions, seminars, workshops, luncheon or dinner programs with a good speaker. An old-timer who had been highly successful for many years gave me, a newcomer, advice I've never forgotten: "Ride the Coattails of Organized Effort."

_____ *Making the Decision* _____

If you feel you have what it takes to manage a real estate office, with experience in the field and aptitude for developing skills in new areas, you then have a decision to make about obtaining managerial training in an established firm or going out on your own. You'll have to decide how many hours you can devote to managing, and how long you must continue to list and sell to meet expenses.

Before you decide to own and manage your own firm, you need to estimate the costs, obtain the necessary financing, determine your company structure, and write out your objectives, a plan for achieving them, and a basic policy and procedure guide. These are covered in subsequent chapters.

Summary

The owner/manager must acquire the knowledge and skills to enable him or her to make decisions that achieve the company goal of making a profit.

*Graduate Realtors Institute®, Certified Residential Specialist®, Certified Real Estate Brokerage Manager®, Certified Commercial-Investment Member®, Master Appraisal Institute®, Residential Manager®, Certified Property Manager®, Counsellor in Real Estate®.

It is not enough for a good owner/broker/manager to stay on top of day-to-day events and make short-term plans. Smart managers study trends that can have impact several years later and make today's decisions with an awareness of what will foster future growth and success.

A great deal of material will be on your desk for you to read and absorb, much of it concerning current situations and future trends. Key information should be conveyed to all in the office.

Remember that the property owner is your client, that a prospect is a customer, and that all the members of the Multiple Listing Service become *subagents of your firm* for the sale of any property under a written agreement.

Learning never ends for those who wish to advance, and ample opportunities exist. Professional designations are worth working for. Public awareness of and demand for high standards of performance from members of the real estate industry are increasing.

Review Questions

1. List three basic principles of real estate office management.

2. Why should an office have a policy and procedure manual?

3. Should a manager have more ego drive than a salesperson? Why or why not?

4. What do associates expect from management?

5. Name three advantages of belonging to a local board of Realtors®, the state association, and the National Association of Realtors®.

6. Why is continuing education important?

2

Your Business Structure

The Form of Organization

You will decide if you wish your company to be a sole proprietorship, a partnership, or a corporation. If incorporated, will you use sub-Chapter S? The decision should be made after consultation with your attorney and your tax advisor.

If you choose to form a partnership, there are the advantages of shared responsibility, more time off for vacations, and coverage in the event of illness. However, difficulties can arise when two strong-minded, independent entrepreneurs get together. If a partnership is planned, be sure there is agreement on basic philosophy, policies, and procedures. Establish areas of authority to be assigned to each. For example, one may be skillful in recruiting and interviewing, the other in training. One may have a flair for advertising, the other for recordkeeping. In the event a conflict of opinions should arise, it may be helpful in preventing a stalemate if it has been arranged that each partner is to have decision-making authority in specific areas. Put your agreement in writing and have an attorney draft it. Include a "buy-out" provision in case the partners split up. Partners may wish life insurance policies that would enable one to buy out the other's interest in the event of death.

You can be incorporated even if you own all the shares of stock. You will then be an employee of the corporation, as president, with salary, withholding taxes, social security deductions, etc. But there are pension plans and other employee benefits. For example, the company can own or lease a car for you, and pay for medical insurance, life insurance, and even your medical bills, in addition to your business travel expenses. Get professional advice on what is best for you.

Broker–Associate Agreement

Will your associates be employees or independent contractors? Most prefer the independent contractor status, which leaves them free to choose their own methods for achieving results. They are not required to keep specific office hours or attend office meetings. You will evaluate performance on results, not methods, and retain or terminate on that basic. You may strongly suggest ways they can achieve good results, and if you are a respected leader, they will probably do it your way. But the choice is theirs.

Some brokers prefer an employer–employee relationship because it gives management control of associates' time and work methods. Much can be required, rather than recommended.

It is possible to have both employees and independent contractors in the same organization. Also an associate may be both self-employed in listing and selling and salaried for administrative duties.

Whether the broker–associate relationship is one of independent contractor or of employer–employee, or a combination of the two, there should be a written agreement clearly understood and *adhered* to by both parties. Have your attorney prepare a suitable agreement.

Independent Contractors

Participation can be *suggested* but not required of an independent contractor in the following activities:

- Participating in a training program
- Putting in office "floor time" or "opportunity time"
- Attending or holding open houses
- Attending office meetings
- Consulting the broker on vacation schedules
- Adhering to procedures in listing and selling

As an independent contractor, an associate will personally pay:

- All license fees
- All membership fees and dues to organizations
- All car and other expenses

Fringe benefits available to independent contractors may include:

- Group medical plan (premium paid entirely by the associate)
- Keogh or IRA retirement plan
- Sales aids such as maps, brochures, pens, etc., paid for by the company

The broker will file IRS Forms 1099* and 1096, with a copy of the salesperson's 1099 Form accompanying the 1096 Form. Copies must be supplied to the independent contractor who will report this information on his or her personal 1040 tax return and who will also file and pay Social Security Self-Employment Tax. He or she is also required to file a Federal Declaration of Estimated Tax each year and to make quarterly payments.

Two forms are recommended that clarify the independent contractor status. One is an affidavit, one a tax declaration. Both should be completed annually, signed by associates, and kept on file. (See Appendix.)

Employer–Employee

If the relationship is one of employer–employee, the management can *require*:

- Participating in specific hours of training
- Taking special courses
- Keeping specific office hours
- Attending and holding open houses
- Attending office meetings
- Performing managerial tasks
- Following specific procedures in listing and selling

Among the fringe benefits that are possible under the employee status are:

- Titles (vice-president, manager, etc.)
- Group medical and life insurance
- Pension and retirement plans
- Reimbursement for auto and other expenses
- Provision of business cards
- A telephone or other credit cards

The employee may be salaried; the independent contractor receives commissions only.

Under an employer–employee agreement, the broker has specific tax obligations and will incur greater bookkeeping expenses.

Payroll records must be accurate, appropriate taxes must be withheld for IRS, and Social Security payments must be made for each employee.

Federal forms the employer will be required to file include:

---

*The same 1099 Form is supplied to all cooperating brokers to whom you paid listing or referral fees.

941 — Quarterly form covering income and Social Security taxes withheld from the employee plus the employer's FICA contribution, accompanied by a check covering both. However, any time the total of these items equals $200, a deposit must be made in the bank using deposit form 501.

940 — Annual return covering Federal Unemployment Tax, which is entirely the employer's expense—no withholding from employee.

W-2 — Annual report of earnings for the year, given to the employee and also furnished to the IRS. This also shows deductions made for Social Security and income tax withholding.

W-3 — Form filed by the employer with the W-2 forms when they are forwarded to IRS.

State tax laws vary as to requirements, so consult your tax accountant.

Legal Advice

You should have a good relationship with an attorney whom you feel free to call whenever a problem arises. You may wish to establish an annual retainer fee. Partners may wish to have different attorneys. Management should always reserve the right to decide when to go to court to collect a commission, but keep your attorney posted on a situation long before it might become a court case.

In the event you do find yourself in court, the careful records you have kept can be a key factor in winning your case.

Legal forms can be purchased at stationary stores, but are best prepared by an attorney. However, two forms it may be helpful to keep on hand are a Power of Attorney and a Promissory Note. Samples are included in the Appendix. Remember that each state has its own laws, and any document must apply to the state where it will be used. When you are determining what will be necessary in the state where a real estate document will be used, remember it will be the state where the *real property* is located.

Criteria for Selecting an Attorney

- *Accessibility*: Can he or she be reached if problems arise evenings or weekends? Whom do you consult if your attorney is away on vacation?

- *Brightness*: You need a wide-awake attorney who is aware of new laws in the real estate and tax fields, who is aware of cases comparable to one you may have, and who is generally well informed about your marketing area.

- *Compatibility*: Can you have an easy, friendly relationship with this attorney?

One assumes that the attorney you select is knowledgeable, thorough, and competent. Compare your personalities. A broker who has a tendency to be avant garde, and perhaps reckless, may need an attorney with a much more conservative viewpoint. A person hesitant about making decisions or taking risks may need a more aggressive attorney. Or you may prefer someone who has the same approach to problem solving that you do. In making decisions it's important to be aware of *all of your options*, and an attorney with a different personality may come up with some options you haven't thought of.

Don't hesitate to change lawyers if your first choice isn't satisfactory. It's important that you feel good about the assistance available to you.

Make it clear what you expect of your attorney and find out what is expected of you.

_____ *Criteria for Selecting a Certified Public Accountant* _____

- *Knowledgeability of the real estate field*: Talk to other brokers he or she works for; get their opinion.
- *Availability*: For consultation if tax problems arise, either for you or your client; for an audit of your tax return.
- *Personality*: Is this someone you are comfortable working with?

CPA's vary in their approach to business endeavors. The most conservative will never chance taking a deduction for an expense that might be questioned and "result in an audit by Internal Revenue Service." Others may feel that the item is a legitimate business expense, take it as a deduction, and be present if IRS does decide to audit your return.

If you are audited, you or the person who prepared the tax return must be able to substantiate that all income was reported and that all expense items have invoices and cancelled checks to prove they were paid, and be prepared to discuss with the field agent (or a supervisor) any deductions that are questioned.

For example, the IRS questioned the deducting of expenses for a broker's trip to a National Associaton of Realtors® convention in Hawaii. The broker was accompanied by his wife, who was in charge of entertainment in their hotel suite. Every night they has a "hospitality suite" and invited a number of brokers. Because actual business (company profits) did result from the contacts made through these endeavors, the expenses were partially allowed.

This example of a bright CPA happened at a Women's Council Luncheon where he spoke. When panty hose first came on the market, they were expensive. Because no self-respecting female associate would wear hose with runs or snags in them (which are easy to get climbing up a ladder in an unfinished house), an associate asked the speaker if panty hose could be deducted as a business expense on Schedule C. The quick-thinking CPA said, "Yes, if they are stamped on the seat with your company name and phone number, they may be allowable as a deduction under advertising!"

Notary Public

It is usually a simple procedure to obtain the license and seal to be a notary public. It's a nice service for you to provide for sellers and buyers. Your availability as a notary on evenings and weekends will help because that's when clients cannot sign papers because the bank, attorney's office, city hall, etc., are closed.

Your own associates may need the services of a notary from time to time. A property owner may need a power of attorney or title papers for the transfer of a car notarized.

Consider offering this service, at no charge, to your clients.

Part-Time Associates

According to the IRS, the definition of a *part-time employee* is someone who works less than 1,000 hours in any one calendar or fiscal year.

One of the questions that always comes up at my management seminars is this: Should we have part-time associates? My standard reply is "It depends."

Part-time associates may be moonlighting school teachers seeking extra income from weekend work in real estate. They may be airline pilots who fly only 10 days a month and are available the other 20 days for real estate. They may have a full-time job in another field and want to "try" real estate before making a full-time commitment.

Your primary concern is that your clients and customers be well served by your firm. Who will care for a seller or buyer when your part-time associate is not available?

Some part-timers are willing to do field work (cold canvassing for listings, for example) that other associates do not do. But if a part-time associate obtains a listing over the weekend, who services that client when he or she is not available weekdays?

You have two options:

1. The manager or assistant manager services all sellers and buyers obtained by the part-time associate and is compensated by a share of the associate's percentage of the listing or selling fee.

2. The "buddy system" is used where the part-timer has an agreement with another associate for services, and they pro-rate the fees earned on a time-shared basis.

Your full-time associate, who is available six or seven days a week, may resent servicing sellers or buyers for a part-time associate unless compensated for time and effort.

Weekends, Holidays, and Time Off

We all need rest from the pressure-cooker demands of a real estate career. Each associate usually chooses a day off, and other associates cover. Weekend office coverage can be rotated so that associates know when they are free — free for a football game, a dinner party, a weekend holiday.

Vacations are important, too. A big advantage to being an independent contractor is that he or she can choose when, where, and for how long to vacation. I recommend winter vacations as well as summer holidays. Each associate can fully enjoy a vacation when arrangements have been made to share the servicing of sellers and buyers with another member of the team.

It is usually not feasible for the manager to take over for each associate when that person is not available. The associates' "buddy system" should prevail.

Summary

Owning and managing a real estate office requires you to make many decisions: whether to incorporate, whether associates are to be employees or independent contractors, what fringe benefits can be offered, etc. Consulting your attorney and your accountant as you make these decisions is time and money well invested.

Knowledge of all the laws that govern the real estate industry is essential. Awareness of all the current trends is also vital. As a business grows, new decisions confront the manager. Assuming you have a positive attitude toward people and service, acquiring the knowledge and skills to succeed in a highly competitive field is a life-long educational process.

Review Questions

1. Discuss five tasks that can be required of an employee but not of an independent contractor.

2.   Who should decide when to consult an attorney at the firm's expense?

3.   List three qualities you would look for in choosing an attorney.

4.   How does the IRS define a part-time employee?

5.   What fringe benefits may be offered to employees?

6.   What retirement plans are available for self-employed persons?

7.   What would you expect a CPA to do for the firm?

8.   Should the manager take over listing and selling appointments whenever an associate is not available? Why or why not?

3

Your Job As Manager

Stepping into the management role and mastering the necessary skills can be very rewarding. Business enterprises, like neighborhoods, rarely remain static. They either increase in value or decline. Your effectiveness as a manager is readily measured by company performance. Winning teams usually have the best coaches.

The manager's role includes —

1. Recruiting associates.
2. Interviewing and qualifying each.
3. Selecting the best candidates.
4. Training associates.
5. Helping associates set and achieve goals.
6. Maintaining a pleasant office atmosphere.
7. Supervising controls: records, budget, etc.
8. Planning office meetings.
9. Establishing basic policies and procedures.
10. Creating effective marketing programs.
11. Retaining good associates.
12. Terminating the nonachievers.
13. Making decisions.
14. Planning for company growth.

These tasks require organizing skill. Your awareness of changing times and needs, and your willingness to be flexible, to take risks, to make decisions are all key factors that will stimulate success. Management need not be a dull desk job, but a stimulating, creative one.

Here are suggestions that can help with your basic tasks.

Recruiting Associates

Reputation. It is a compliment when potential associates come to you seeking affiliation. Even though you are fully staffed, ask them to fill out an application and keep it on file. A thank you for their interest is in order, and it's a comfortable feeling to have a resource file of potential associates.

Newspaper Advertising. If you choose this medium, use a box number, not your name. Request that résumés be sent to the box, and you can avoid wasting hours interviewing potentially unsuitable applicants or ones you have already turned down.

Word of Mouth. Your friends and associates will suggest possibilities. Encourage them to do so when you need another associate.

New Licensees. Ask instructors of prelicensing courses in your area to recommend qualified students to you.

Students. Contact the colleges and universities in your area that offer real estate courses. Ask instructors to refer graduates to you.

Your objective in recruiting is to obtain a *quantity* of candidates so you can sift for *quality*. In trade jargon, a "body shop" is an office that takes on any licensee who walks in the door. Your skill in recruiting will enable you to select only top-notch personnel. This will reduce turnover, increase profits, and save many management headaches.

Interviewing Applicants

Initial Interview

This may be brief. You thank each for coming in and provide an application form. You may wish to discuss some of your company policies; if you plan to test promising applicants, say so. If you are not adding to your staff at present but consider the person a good potential associate based on your first meeting and the information on the application form, let the person know you'll call when there is an opening.

In interviewing if you ask open-ended questions, you'll get a lot more information that if you ask close-ended questions (see "One-to-One Counselling" in Chapter 13). During the interview observe the general health and degree of enthusiasm of the applicant.

Nowadays there is an increasing number of nonsmokers. If the applicant is a smoker, ask if it would bother him or her to not smoke when in a car with customers, at a client's home, or in the office if most are nonsmokers.

You will have noted if the applicant was on time for the appointment and, of course, will inquire into noncareer demands on his or her time. Look for clues as to ability to organize time.

Always ask the applicant why he or she wants to embark on a real estate career. Sample replies include:

- "I love people."
- "I like houses."
- "I'm bored as a housewife."
- "I can make more money than I can by selling shoes."
- "It's one field I can get into that pays a lot, where I don't need a college education."
- "We've bought and sold a lot of houses and think we know more than most brokers."
- "My children are all in school and I want to work, but need a job with flexible hours."
- "I'm in a dead-end job and tired of being transferred. We'd like to put down roots in this community."
- "I want to make money, but I only want to work at a part-time job."
- "My father's in real estate out in Des Moines, Iowa. He thinks I should go into it."

The answers actually tell you a lot about the personality and motivation of the applicant. If you feel the person is not suitable for your office, advise him or her of this decision tactfully.

Second Interview

This will be an in-depth interview with promising applicants. You want to know a lot about them; they want to know a lot about the company. Set aside at least an hour and avoid interruptions. Inquire about their past successful enterprises including high school activities. Ask how their family feels about mother or father having a real estate career in view of long and odd hours, evening and weekend work, and uncertain income.

- What are their income needs and expectations?
- What sacrifices are they willing to make to achieve their goals?
- How do they feel about continuing education?

Emphasize the importance of being a good team player, and outline your expectations. Share your policy and procedure manual, explain what the company will provide to assist them in becoming successful and what your training program covers.

Testing

Because a personal interview is subjective, testing is recommended to help you decide on promising applicants. While no test can guarantee career success, tests are an objective tool that can assist you in the decision-making process. A test will indicate job suitability.

Remember, an empty desk will cost you less in lost business than an ineffectual or untrainable associate.

For example, the "Real Estate Personality Dynamics Inventory" is available from the Marketing Survey and Research Corp., Research Park, P.O. Box 2050, Princeton, New Jersey 08540. It takes about an hour for an associate to complete, it costs less than $100, and the results will be reported within a week. It measures ego drive, empathy, and appropriate skills for a career in real estate. Share the inventory with the applicant and explore strengths and weaknesses.

Other tests available include some that can be evaluated by you as soon as they are completed by the applicant. When you buy the test forms, you'll receive instructions for administration and evaluation. These can be less expensive and faster, but your evaluation may be less objective than that of a professional in the field of testing.

Following are some examples of test results I've experienced or heard about from other brokers:

- An inventory indicated high intelligence and a dedication to service and teamwork, but did not recommend for real estate as "too much empathy, not enough ego drive." The applicant went into real estate, was not successful, changed to social work and is very successful.

- A report on another applicant stated that the person had a tendency to talk too much, and unless this could be curbed, he would talk himself right out of a close. When he was unable to achieve results in real estate, he changed careers and is successful in another field where a tendency to talk too much is not a detriment.

- For a person I liked very much, the report came back "not recommended". Reasons given were the person's need for structure and security. I regretfully declined the application and she joined another firm. After a year of hard work and zero results, she obtained a well-paid job as an executive secretary and is much happier in her new role.

Test designers and evaluators do not claim 100 percent accuracy, but in the majority of cases predictions work out. There will be exceptions, of course. I've had brokers tell me their top producer was only "mildly recommended" or "not recommended". Another told me she took on a "highly recommended" who was hopeless on the job and soon changed careers. But none of the applicants I've tested, and declined, has done well in the field, although most were taken on by other brokers.

After you have the inventory evaluation to review, you still have a decision to make in which the test is only factor.

Selecting

Why do so many persons choose each year to embark on a career in real estate? (More than 250,000 new licensees!)

What does it take to succeed?

- A willingness to work hard without an immediate pay-out for the work.
- An ability to plan and organize work days.
- An aptitude for learning.
- A desire for self growth.

Why do so many "drop out" of the field?

- A lack of awareness of what's required to become productive.
- No opportunity to participate in a training program.
- A low tolerance for frustration.
- An unwillingness to actively seek prospects and cultivate referrals.
- A lack of interest in ongoing educational opportunities.

Some people ask if women make better sales agents than men in the residential field. It's the person that counts, not the gender. If a woman does not have to support herself or a family, she may be able to stay in the business, with little income, for the time it takes to achieve good results. But she may have more demands on her time from children than a man has.

Another question that comes up is age. Is someone in his twenties too young? In his fifties too old? Don't be prejudiced against any age group; all have potential. In fact, don't be prejudiced. One broker told me she would never take on an overweight associate; another told me his top producer is rolypoly, but cheerful, fun, and very successful.

Are extroverts more likely to succeed than introverts? Ask several managers if any of their top producers are more introverted than extroverted and the responses may surprise you. Introverts tend to give more attention to follow-ups, have more patience with time-consuming details, and do very well.

One of the traps it is easy to fall into in selecting a new associate is that of choosing someone very much like ourselves. We recognize that we feel very comfortable with the person; they seem to have the same attitudes, interests, and strengths. We tend to overlook the fact that they may also possess our same weak points, and that many of the characteristics we like do not really relate to the job they will be doing. A good baseball team encompasses a variety of skills and would be unlikely to win many games if all were super pitchers or hitters.

TABLE 3-1   CHECKLIST BEFORE SELECTING

	Yes	No
1. Are the applicant's appearance and personality pleasing?		
2. Will this person fit into our office and be an asset?		
3. Did the references on the application check out favorably?		
4. Was the applicant responsive to our discussion of office policies and procedures?		
5. Is the person willing to invest time and effort?		
6. Can the applicant survive if he has no income for three months? For six months?		
7. Did the inventory indicate healthy ego drive? Good empathy?		
8. Has the applicant joined community organizations and taken on responsibilities?		
9. Does the person have a positive attitude toward training?		
10. Is he or she interested in ongoing education?		

If 8 out of 10 answers are "YES", you've made a good choice.

Training

While a large firm may have a full-time trainer, the average small office relies on the manager for this job. A big advantage of joining a franchise is the professional training provided. As a task of the manager, it's usually one-to-one training. This is expensive in terms of the time consumed, but the training will pay off in the new associate's production if done effectively. Plan and write a specific training program. Guidelines are set out in Chapter 6. Supplement this by encouraging the associate to take educational courses available, such as those that the Realtors National Marketing Institute® sponsor.

Goal Setting

A major management task is goal setting, both for the firm as a whole and for each associate. (See Chapter 4.)

The manager—

- Sets company goals for the year and writes out a plan to achieve them.
- Puts the plan into action.
- Measures the results.
- Compares expectations with results.
- Reviews on a monthly or quarterly basis.
- Revises when indicated.

No one goes after a goal he doesn't really want. Translate desires into specifics. If the associate sets $15,000 as a desirable income figure, is a portion to used for a new car? A child's college education? A bigger house? A luxury vacation, or what?

Your own experience in writing out goals for the company will help you in counselling associates with their personal goal setting. If a trainee sets too high an income goal, it's your job to point out what is realistic and achievable in the current year. When an experienced associate sets a goal that you consider too low, encourage the associate to strive for a higher return on his or her proven ability.

What's worth doing is worth measuring, so review goals and progress to date with your associates on a regular basis.

Retention

The ability to retain valuable associates is one hallmark of a good manager. Associates are likely to remain where there is—

- A friendly atmosphere to work in.
- A favorable image of the firm.
- An opportunity for excellent income.
- Pride in belonging to a successful company.
- Praise for work well done.

One method used by some firms to retain good producers is a sliding scale for their share of the commissions earned. For example, if each associate's share of the basic budget or "desk cost" is $15,000 a year, all fees earned after that amount may be split with a higher percentage to the associate and a lesser one to the company. But don't risk a bonus or profit-sharing plan that would infringe on an associate's status a an independent contractor.

What may be a fine incentive plan for an employee may be a "no-no" for an independent contractor.

Recognition of achievement can be expressed by "Million Dollar Club" plaques or jewelry which are tangible symbols of success. If the average-priced house in the area were $100,000, it would take 10 listings that were sold or 10 sales to qualify for the award. Some form of recognition helps motivate and retain good producers. It may be one red rose or a basket of apples that appears on the top producer's desk each month.

Turnover

Some turnover is essential to success: the poor producers or office problem makers should be weeded out and replaced. Too much turnover is destructive of office morale and expected profits, and is a symptom of poor management.

National estimates of turnover rate range from 30 to 70 percent. Unfortunately, the higher statistics largely reflect new agents who try real estate for a few months, do not succeed, and change careers. Poor selection processes, inadequate training, and lack of supervision were probably the causes. Perhaps the associate had unreasonable expectations of immediate earnings and did not stay in the field long enough to become productive.

Determine what a healthy percentage of turnover is for your company and be alert for new potential.

Termination

The least liked task of most managers is terminating the nonproductive or troublemaking associate. It's ego threatening to the manager ("I made a poor choice"). The person who is unable to reach individual and company goals may be a good friend and a well-liked person in the office. You hate to see yourself as ruthless or solely profit oriented. But a basic management function is to weed out and terminate the inept and replace poor achievers with good ones.

Be aware when it's time to sever the relationship; do it with compassion but firm intent. Don't be talked out of it by a hard luck story. Both parties will feel better with a clean break.

When an associate leaves for whatever reason, keep the arrangement friendly but businesslike. Immediately go over all listing and prospect files. Agree on which clients and prospects will be retained by your office and assigned to other associates and which will be serviced by the associate who is leaving. On business that went into a listing or sale contract while the associate was affiliated with you, your firm is entitled to the office share of commission when the transaction is completed. Make a list of those accounts where you expect to be recognized and see that both the associate and his new head of office understand the policy and procedure and have a copy of the list.

Protecting Your Investment in Training

A broker makes a major investment in the team he or she recruits, trains, and coaches to success. But competition grows ever fiercer, and the easy way for a new office in town to make profits quickly is to raid existing firms for qualified personnel.

How can the broker who has spent a great deal of time and effort in training a new associate protect that investment?

In *Real Estate Today* magazine (October 1980, p. 62), William D. North, senior vice president and general counsel for the National Association of Realtors®, suggests a 90-day cooling-off provision in the written agreement between broker and salesperson. He suggests that this paragraph be included in the agreement:

> Salesperson agrees to notify broker in writing of his intention to terminate this agreement not less than ninety days prior to the effective date of such termination unless such termination is for breach of this agreement and broker has refused or failed to cure such breach within ten days after written notification of it. It is mutually agreed that in the event salesperson fails to give the notice of termination required herein, broker shall, as liquidated damages and not as a penalty, be entitled to retain all commissions earned or due salesperson from broker but unpaid as of the date of his termination or accruing thereafter under the terms of this agreement.

Making Decisions

Typical of decisions the manager will be called upon to make are some of the following real-life case studies:

- The top producer tells you that because he is consistently number one in listings and sales, he should get a bigger split on commissions than the other associates do.

- You need another associate in your office and get an application from one who is now a top-notch producer with another firm. Her track record checks out, but she feels that all commissions should be split 60/40, not 50/50, and if you are not willing to change your office policy on this, she won't move to your firm.

- Your office sells a house that was listed by another broker. The listing stated that the property consisted of one acre or more. At the closing the deed conveyed only seven-tenths of an acre. The buyer objected, demanding a reduced price; the seller refused to negotiate; and the associate called the manager.

- Terry is a high-income producer in listings and sales but dislikes details, paperwork, and follow-through. He tends to misplace keys, he loses files, and he overbooks appointments. He has super energy, but makes demands on other associates. The others complain to management.

- Chris has been with the firm for three years and works hard. She's the bottom producer despite good work habits, attitude, and skill. Chris has been unable to earn enough to meet desk costs.

What do you, the manager, do? When problems arise, "the buck stops here" — squarely on the manager's desk. The job of training never ends; new information must constantly be absorbed and communicated. A good sense of humor is a manager's much needed attribute as you strive to live up to the motto "Be Graceful Under Pressure."

Some of the problems you'll be confronted with as an owner/broker/manager involve sellers, buyers, renters, and lawyers, as well as your associates. The following cases occurred in our area:

Wells That Go Dry

An older couple sold a large home to a family who moved in with four children. Within a month, the well went dry; they had no water, and spent nearly $10,000 replacing the well. The prior owners had moved to a condominium unit in a nearby town; the buyers sued the sellers and the broker. The listing information given to the purchasers had simply been "Drilled well, 100 feet deep. Owner states has ample water supply." The court found neither were guilty because the water supply had been adequate for the prior owners, although insufficient for a large family.

In another case, a young couple bought a modest cottage in the fall. When summer came, the well went dry. Information on the listing had been "Dug well, about 30 feet deep. Owners state adequate supply." Borrowing water and a hose from a neighbor, the new owner learned that "This happens every summer; I always gave them water until it rained a lot." The couple demanded that the broker replace the well. The broker refused because all information obtainable had been disclosed. The new well was paid for by the owner. It was a major property improvement, and this was reflected in the resale value.

The third case cost the broker and the associate money. At the time they purchased an almost-new vacant house, the buyers asked the associate if they should have a building inspection. The associate replied, "Why spend the money? The seller says that the builder's warranties will be in effect for another 10 months." When the purchasers moved in, there was no water. The well was defective, and the pump broken by sand being brought up from the dry well. Meanwhile, because the builder had gone into bankruptcy, no warranties were being honored, and the seller had moved out of the state. The distressed buyers complained that had they been advised to have a building inspection, the defect could have been discovered. The company and the associate shared the expense of a new pump and well. It cost a lot more than the commission earned, but it won good friends.

The Tenants Who Couldn't Pay Rent

When Mr. and Mrs. R rented the house, their references and credentials were excellent. Then he lost his job, became despondent, couldn't get a job, and couldn't pay rent. He had a large dog, got a gun, and wouldn't allow an agent on the property. The broker notified the authorities, and the renters were evicted after due notice. The house was a mess and the owner complained. The broker paid to have the house cleaned up, broken windows replaced, etc., and refunded the rental commission. Good will—but at a price!

The Couple Who Paid Cash

A young couple was enthusiastic about renting a furnished house for the winter, while the owners were in Florida. References were requested and obtained. Their bank statement had a healthy four-figure balance, although it was a fairly recent account. They said that they had been living in Europe. A purported former landlord said that they were excellent tenants. The man claimed to be an artist, and an art gallery wrote (on letterhead that turned out to be phony) that it purchased his paintings regularly. So leases were drawn and signed, and the rent and security deposit were paid in cash from a big bankroll in the young man's pocket. They moved in, they were "quiet neighbors" according to later police reports, and they moved out—with a van full of all the household furnishings! The owners, returning to an empty house, were in a state of shock and felt that the broker was responsible. The broker, having taken the normal precaution of obtaining references on the tenant, did not feel responsible. The police were unable to track down the young couple. Fortunately, the owners' insurance policy replaced most of their losses.

The Unpleasant Tenant

The owner's corporation transferred him overseas for two years, and he rented his home furnished. Mr. and Mrs. Z moved in and began a steady stream of complaints. They made several calls a day to the associate at the office and calls late at night to the associate's home: "The stove thermostat was not accurate, a shower head was clogged, a bathtub faucet leaked, we need a new fluorescent light fixture, the outside doors are not weather-stripped, the lawnmower doesn't do a good job, etc." After several months of contacting workmen, obtaining estimates, and getting the owner's approval of the repair expenses, the badgered associate said to the manager, "I give up! I won't take any more of these complaining phone calls!" Then the tenants refused to pay rent, on the grounds that the house was not satisfactory. The owner was informed and said, "Get those dreadful people out of my house." The broker, after consulting an attorney, wrote the tenants that the owner was sorry that they weren't satisfied with the property, pointed out that "there is no such thing as a perfect house, completely flaw-free", and stated that the owner was willing to release the renters from the balance of the lease if they wished to vacate the premises.

The renters paid up and shut up, but not without some parting phone calls to the broker, threatening to write the real estate licensing commission and have the broker's license revoked. The broker dryly responded with "Let me give you their address and zip code." That ended the case.

The Missing Sign

A charming old house came on the market and generated a lot of interest. Beside the front door was a plaque "Circa 1849". The purchasers loved antiques and were delighted to find a 125-year-old house. However, on the day of the closing, the little old black and gold sign proclaiming the age of the house was missing. The sellers had already moved out of the state and were represented at the closing by their attorney. The buyers came to the closing and asked about the missing sign. Their attorney, studying the title search, said, "But the house was built in 1927!" (It was later learned that the sellers always bought older houses and put their "Circa" sign up.) The buyers protested that they didn't want a house that wasn't a genuine antique and accused the broker of misrepresentation. The closing was recessed while the broker arranged financing; then a closing took place with the title transferred to the broker. The would-be purchasers were released from the contract and all monies refunded. Later the broker sold them a truly old house. The broker's wife, who had excellent taste, renovated the "Circa 1849" house with paint and wallpaper, and refinished the floors, and the broker was able to sell it at a profit, listed at its proper age!

In this case, rather than getting involved with a possible lawsuit and losing the good will of the buyer, the broker chose to purchase the property, fix it up, and resell it — a wise choice, as events proved.

The Transferred Seller

Under his employer's relocation plan, the seller had 30 days to try to sell his house before transferring it to a Third Party Relocation Firm at their appraised price. He listed it with us for the 30 days. Near the end of that marketing time we had an interested buyer and were negotiating offers and counteroffers. We needed more time to finalize a sale. If the seller signed the Third Party contract, the property would be off the market for a week or so, pending paperwork, and then might be listed by another office. What would you do if this happens to you? You can call the relocation director of the seller's company and explain the situation, giving facts on the buyer, the offers, and the counteroffers. Request a week's extension in listing time, so that you can finalize the purchase agreement. You can also call the Third Party firm to request an immediate, even if temporary extension of your listing so that you do not lose the prospective buyer or your listing fee. We made the sale!

The Angry Buyer

A seller, advised that his property should sell in the $95,000 to $100,000 price range, argued that it was worth more and listed at $125,000. After months of little activity, he began to reduce his price, dropping month by month to $120,000, $115,000, $112,000, $110,000, $105,000. An associate whose listing book had not been brought up to date showed it to a prospect who liked the house. The associate quoted the listed price at $110,000. The buyer offered $100,000, and the owner accepted. A few months after the closing, when a neighbor asked what he had paid, the buyer learned that the asking price had been $105,000 at the time that he had submitted the offer. He wrote an angry letter to the associate demanding that the commission be paid to him. The upset associate turned the letter, and later phone calls, over to the manager. The manager tried to assure the buyer that he had paid fair market value and even offered (in writing) to buy the house from Mr. Angry at the price paid. Mr. Angry responded by notifying the state real estate license commission that he felt damaged and that the broker's license should be revoked. The commission investigated the case and replied that the house had been purchased under list price, but that if the buyer was dissatisfied with the property, the broker would return the purchase money upon transfer of title. The case was dismissed, but no friends were gained, through an associate's oversight in not keeping his listing book 100 percent accurate!

The Greedy Seller

Most sellers recognize the value of your services, appreciate a good marketing job, and pay the fee for the services done. Occasionally, greed enters the picture.

Mr. S accepted an offer to purchase and agreed to the terms and contingencies, but while the contracts were being drawn by his attorney, he received a higher offer. He told the first would-be buyer that he was backing out. This upset person called the associate who had negotiated the agreement and threatened to sue all involved. The associate asked the manager what to do. The manager called the firm's attorney who expressed the viewpoint that while the seller had a moral obligation to the first buyer, he might not have a legal one—but it was time to "rattle the sabers." After consulting with the upset buyer's attorney and the seller's attorney, the matter was resolved. Rather than risk having the property tied up in litigation for a year or more, the seller decided to go through with his original agreement.

The Tricky Seller

Mr. S's property had been on the market for nearly six months when a ready, willing, and able buyer submitted an offer. When terms were agreed upon, the seller said that he would draw up his own contract of sale. There was a week's delay, and when a copy of the contract arrived at the broker's office, a key sentence had been crossed out on the stationery store form—namely, the sentence calling for payment of a commission to the sales agent. The associate called this omission to the seller's attention. The seller said, "Your listing expired while the contracts were being drawn, and with no signed listing in effect, you are not entitled to a commission." The associate turned the problem over to the manager, who called the company's attorney. A decision was made to sue the seller for the commission, and the case was resolved in the broker's favor.

Summary

Your willingness and ability to set goals for the company help the associates set individual goals. As a manager you are a recruiter, a personnel manager, and a trainer, among other things.

As a manager, you must be a good leader. You will be directing the collected energy of a group of individuals in a sustained community where their personal contribution of energy and endeavor results in success for the whole.

Managers are constantly confronted with decision making. Weigh the facts, make your decision, and implement it. "Speak softly, but carry clout!"

You need credibility with the group, which generates confidence, the ability to communicate, and commitment to *their* collective energy. If the manager withdraws his or her interest and energy from the team, they may withdraw their energy. The manager's attitude strongly influences the office climate. If you are enthusiastic, sincere, responsive, fair, and encouraging, you can sustain a pleasant business atmosphere in which all can work for the common good.

Your business will not grow on the strength of your name, personality, or bank account. It will grow if you are aware of your goals, responsive to people, and sincerely interested in servicing their needs.

Review Questions

1. List ten functions of a manager.
2. List five ways to recruit associates.
3. Role-play an interview with an applicant.
4. Discuss what testing can and cannot do.
5. List five factors that a manager will consider in selecting an associate.
6. What are the advantages of a good training program?
7. List three criteria for goal setting.
8. Discuss the factors that would influence a manager in deciding to terminate an associate's affiliation with the firm.
9. List five good causes for termination.
10. Role-play a termination session in which the "actor–manager" has decided to end the relationship and the "actor–associate" is determined to stay on.

4

Goal Setting, Office Meetings, and Motivation

Your market area will usually be the towns covered by your board's Multiple Listing Service. In a large city you may choose to focus on one residential area; Northwest, Southeast, whatever. If you know that there were 500 transactions in this market area last year and you'd like to capture 10 percent of the listings and sales, your objective is 50 of each. If your experience has shown that a good producer will generate 12 to 14 listings and the same number of sales a year, you'll need four good producers to reach your goal.

Remember that goals or objectives must be "D - A - M" good:

D esirable

A chievable

M easurable

Desirable. Desire must be strong, and spelled out. Why do you want to be a leader in your market area? Prestige? Income? If you simply desire to have a comfortable office to spend some hours in every day, acknowledge that and plan accordingly.

Achievable. Your goals must be realistic. To say that as a new firm you intend to be number one in sales in a year would be unrealistic. Desirable, yes, but unlikely. If you figure it's realistic to capture 10 or 20 percent of your marketing area in your first year, that's a valid goal. Increase goals annually as your opportunity for market penetration increases.

Measurable. Make all your goals measurable. Translate goals to numbers: x listings plus x sales = x percent of the market with an estimated income of *x* dollars. Write it down, and develop your plan. Will you aim for four listings and four sales per month? This is a measurable goal. Estimate the average listing and selling fees in your market area so you can plan your budget.

In addition, they must be *written down*. Once written, goals work on you as you work on the goals.

Company Goal Plan

Write out a plan to reach the goal you have established. How many salespersons will it take to achieve this goal? In your market area do associates list and sell one per month? Or two? Price tends to determine this factor: in an area where the average price of houses ranges from $35,000 to $45,000, good producers may average two listings and two sales per month. When properties approach the $80,000 to $100,000 price range, listing and sales volume may be one each per month per associate.

You can estimate the average price range in your market area (Board MLS statistics and Commercial Record files are helpful). You know the average number of properties that change title in a year. After deciding what percentage of your potential market you plan to capture, determine how many associates you will need to achieve your goal—two, three, four, or more? Can you attract, train, and supervise that number?

Do you plan to list and sell yourself? Many managers wear too many hats and defeat company goals by trying to do it all. My recommendation is to phase yourself out gradually as a salesperson and give that time to management.

TABLE 4-1   SAMPLE WRITTEN GOAL AND PLAN

- My market area has a turnover of 400 properties per year.
- The average sale price is $60,000.
- Our office commission rate is 6 percent, or $3,600 per house. This is divided equally between listing and selling offices in most of our area.
- My goal is 10 percent of the market or 40 properties to be listed and 40 to be sold.

40 properties listed	= income of (40 x $1,800)	= $ 72,000
40 properties sold	= income to (40 x $1,800)	= $ 72,000
	Total income expected	= $144,000

- From this gross income, one half is to be paid to sales associates for each listing and sale, or $72,000.
- Leaving for the company, to pay for all overhead plus manager's compensation and company profit $72,000.

Now you have a figure to budget.

An able associate can list and sell one property per month for a gross company income of $3,600. The associate gets $1,800, the office $1,800. This earns the associate $21,600 in commissions for a year, and the same for the office. A top producer may double this income. A beginner may earn half as much.

Analyze your company goals and your staff requirements. Can you attract producers who will generate enough listing and selling fees to pay your overhead? Do you want to start with some experienced associates? How many trainees can you afford to have?

TABLE 4-2 CHECK LIST FOR SETTING COMPANY GOALS
FOR YOUR MARKETING AREA

- Last year _____ properties were listed for sale. We listed _____ properties or _____ percent of these.
- Our roll-over rate on listings was _____ percent. (If you listed 100 and 80 were sold, your roll-over rate is 80 percent.)
- Last year _____ properties were sold. Our company sold _____ properties or _____ percent.
- We had a total of _____ prospects for obtaining listings. We listed _____ for _____ percent capture rate.
- We had a total of _____ prospects for purchasing and sold _____, for a capture rate of _____.
- We sent _____ Referrals Out. Those sold were _____ percent.
- We received _____ Referrals In. We sold _____; our capture rate was _____ percent.
- The number one firm in listings last year was _____. We were number _____.
- The leading firm in sales last year was _____ with _____ sales. We were number _____ with _____ sales.
- Next year we anticipate _____ properties to be listed for sale. We expect to list _____ percent. This averages out to (number of) listings by each associate.
- We expect to sell _____ properties, or _____ per associate.
- If our capture rate averages _____ percent, we will need _____ old and new prospects or _____ per month per associate.
- To increase Referrals Out, each associate needs _____ per month.

Questions to ask:

- Can we obtain more listings? How?
- Can we improve our listing roll-over rate? How?
- Can we sell more properties? How?
- Can we increase Referrals Out and Referrals In?
- What can management do to help achieve individual and company goals?

How long will your bankroll last? With management goals written that are desirable and measurable, you have a focus for your interviewing, selecting, and training process.

Associates' Goals

Ask what an associate expects to earn. If they have experience in the business, check out their track record. If new, describe your training program and expectations. Build your team to achieve the goals you have set.

Acquaint associates with goal setting. Do an X-Factor sheet with them (see the sample in the Appendix). Review it regularly, either monthly or quarterly. There is no growth without struggle; your success will depend on the effort you invest.

Annual Goal Setting

An office meeting in January, or whatever month starts the firm's fiscal year, is important. The purpose is to set company goals for the coming year. It might be called Management Goal setting with the Participation of the Associates, or M-G-P-A.

The agenda would include:

- The manager's summary of total listings and sales in the area; the company percentages.
- Where the company stands compared to competing firms in the number of listings, number of sales, and ratings.
- Setting of objectives for the coming year, to be shared by associates with ideas, discussion, examples, etc.
- Summary of ways suggested to increase income and not increase expenditures.

The point should be made that next year's budget is being set up, based on last year's income from listing and sales, and last year's expenses. Company dollar income and expenses must be projected for next year's budget. Inflation needs to be acknowledged as a factor in planning the budget.

The manager prepares for the meeting by filling in last year's figures and percentages on the Checklist shown above. Associates contribute suggestions for filling in the projected figures for the coming year.

Many of the suggestions will add up to the company spending more money:

- "We should do more advertising."
- "Maybe if we decorated the office . . . ."
- "Why don't we give more parties?"

The manager can counter with, "If we increase our expenditures in these areas, we'll have to eliminate other items from the budget, or increase our income. Many of our expenses are fixed, like rent. Are you willing to cut out secretarial help? Promotional aids? Contributions to local organizations that we make for good community relations?"

The objective of the meeting is twofold:

- Management shares the data on where the company stands in the marketing area.
- Associates share ideas for increasing their productivity and incomes.

Note any remarks that indicate a willingness to achieve more, but don't pin the person down to a commitment in the presence of others. These comments should be covered in your follow-up, one-to-one, goal-setting conference with each associate. Typical remarks may be:

- "I should do a better job of following up my . . . ."
- "I wish I were more aggressive about getting listings."
- "I could be in touch more often with area brokers who send me re-ferrals."

Key words for the manager to use at this meeting, and in the individual, follow-up, goal-setting sessions, are:

- "Why?"   (to clarify the purpose of an action)
- "How?"   (to discuss ways and means)
- "When?" (to agree on a projected date to start action)

Hopefully, they will commit themselves to endeavors that will help them achieve personal and company goals.

The meeting is an opportunity to communicate to all the staff new information, current trends, or a summary of what you, the manager, gleaned from a seminar or national convention you just attended.

Office Meetings

Office meetings, when well planned and led, are a form of ongoing training to help the firm achieve objectives.

While employees can be required to attend meetings, it is optional for independent contractors. And if they feel the meetings are a waste of time, or just "ego trips" for the manager, they attend reluctantly or not at all.

Planning

All meetings need a purpose, an agenda, a convenient time, and a place. Let associates suggest the time, place, and length of meeting they prefer. Schedule them on a regular basis, whether once a week or once a month. What subjects would be of interest to the associate? Teachers do lesson plans before every class—a good manager writes out a meeting plan. One hour is usually long enough; the leader should keep the objective in mind and sum up the meeting while there is still time for any questions.

Try to hold meetings in a comfortable setting, free from interruptions. Have it understood that no axe will drop, no person singled out for blame. We all learn best in a secure setting and friendly atmosphere.

Learning Techniques

Adults are not a "captive audience" as children in a classroom may be. Lecturing is a useful technique in classrooms; it's not the best teaching technique for office meetings. The manager will be a minister for many of the needs of personnel, but should avoid preaching! Workshop techniques are far better learning experiences and encourage involvement.

Some of the techniques a manager can use to make meetings lively are as follows:

- "Town Hall"—to share the concerns of all, then select priorities for discussion.

- "Brain Storm"—a problem is described and several dozen possible solutions are tossed out by associates, striving first for "off the top of your head" quantity, even if it sounds crazy. Then cull for quality. (A pad of newsprint on an easel and a big marker will help the leader jot down all the ideas contributed, then reviewed.)

- "Role-Plays"—These are helpful when the purpose of the meeting is sharpening some specific skill. For example, the stated objective may be "How to overcome buyer objections." *Don't* assign your weakest salesperson to the role of the broker. Let that person play the part of a difficult buyer. Use a top producer in the role of the salesperson. Keep the role-play brief; then ask for *constructive* comments from the others. Applaud your actors.

- "Case Study"—Write out several realistic problems that arise in real estate. Read the problem; let all discuss possible solutions.

- "Buzz Groups"—Even a small office (4 to 10 persons) can separate into "dyads" or "triads", groups of two or three. Each group is assigned a different problem and given 10 to 15 minutes to come up with suggestions. Time is called, and the groups report; comments are invited.

Whatever techniques you decide to use, a good leader encourages participation by all, doesn't let one or two dominate, keeps control by asking good questions, and is a *good listener!*

Bring in a guest speaker occasionally, an expert in a specialized field. While a lawyer, builder, appraiser, and tax accountant are some obvious choices, don't be afraid to try the unusual. At one of our most provocative meetings we had an astrologer who told us the buying motivations of various signs of the zodiac! For example, Scorpio values privacy and tends to prefer offbeat or unconventional properties; a Taurus will look for comfort and prestige, and be willing to "fix up". The stated objective of this meeting was to increase insight into buying motivations and skill in determining "what turns people on".

Some Office Meeting Ideas

Discussion meeting re:

- Policies
- Procedures
- Advertising
- Farming
- Marketing tools
- Annual goal setting

Outside speaker meeting re:

- Financing
- Construction
- Land development
- Investments
- Taxation
- Advertising
- Appraising
- Legal problems
- Commercial property
- Property management
- Condominiums

Office track record and evaluation meeting re:

- How many prospects for listing or sale?
- Source of prospects?

- Results to date?
- Company expectations?
- How to increase prospects?

Skill improvement meeting re:

- Prospecting
- Listing presentations — "If you were required to do nothing but LIST for six months, would you survive? If not, why not?" Emphasize that listings are the highest form of selling. Buyers usually sell themselves. Good brokers list the most properties and control the market area.
- Convincing the seller to price realistically — What tools will you use? Practice a presentation. "We are after Quality Listings, Motivated Seller, Priced Right, with an Exclusive Right to Sell."
- Closing techniques — Overcoming objections, detecting the dominant buying motive or DBM.
- Servicing prospects — List 10 things you can do to generate loyalty from sellers or buyers.
- Negotiating skills
- Converting a rental prospect to a buyer
- Followthrough for seller and buyer after the closing
- Human communication
- Getting repeat and referral business:
- What?
- Why?
- Where?
- When?
- How?

Each should list 10 ways to increase income from referrals. Discuss.

Morale Building

Office meetings are even more important in tough times than in boom years. Associates need reassurance that a recession situation is temporary and they will welcome suggestions to maintain productivity.

Recognizing that economic changes occur periodically, management must be prepared to handle poor marketing conditions with skill. Share with your associates three of the options available to the firm:

- Giving up and getting out of the business.

- Enduring and somehow hanging on until marketing conditions improve.
- Prevailing in spite of economic conditions, continuing to make a profit.

The key ingredient for successful survival in tough times is *attitude!* If the manager is aware that recessions come and go over the years, that boom times also come and go, he or she can generate an attitude of optimism among associates and defeat an attitude of pessimism that could doom the firm to failure.

Communicate your convictions that the situation is temporary, that good times will come again, and stress that there are opportunities to make money even in a "down" market. Associates tend to get bored or restless in times of inactivity, when the phone doesn't ring, ads don't bring response, or would-be buyers shy away from high interest rates. You don't want to lose good producers although it may be a good time to "weed out" poor producers.

The prudent owner will have set aside some funds from high profit years in an interest-bearing "Survival Fund". These monies can tide you over, pay the bills, and keep you going when income is scarce. If you are dunned by the creditors, valuable associates may leave.

Time will be available for creative work, reviewing systems, improving follow-up procedures, and other projects. Some good real estate investments may be available; potential buyers should be contacted and their holdings reviewed.

While the company has certain fixed expenses, like rent, other expenditures can be reduced and some trimming of the budget will help your cash flow position. It's a time to check carefully results from advertising. You need to keep your name before the public, but public relations efforts may be more effective and less costly than some of your customary advertising.

Keep a positive attitude and keep associates busy.

Motivation

Research indicates that contrary to common belief, money is *not* the number one motivator for most associates. The real motivators are these:

- Job satisfaction
- Challenge
- Recognition by peers
- Self achievement

Management's role is to provide the climate and opportunity that will enable associates to grow and develop their potential. Money rewards follow.

Can motivation be applied from without, like a band-aid? We may hear a powerful "motivator" speaker at a convention, but will we change the way we work unless there is a strong motivation to do so within us? Is what motivates Associate A the same as what motivates Associate B? We all have hidden drives. For one it may be security, for another challenge and change.

Testing may reveal some motivations; your own insight will uncover others as you observe the associates' patterns. Carl Rogers said, "The aim in life is to develop one's potential." You can be helpful in this, by sharing your observations. You can strengthen skills in areas they wish to improve. You can be a friendly counselor. But I do not believe you can motivate the unmotivated.

Some may be realistically aware of what keeps them from achieving good production status. "I'm basically lazy," said one frankly. "Do you want to change?" I asked. "Not really," was the reply.

A good leader may inspire change—change in work habits, for example—but the self determination of each individual will decide the outcome.

Summary

Management's major task is to set viable objectives for the firm and see that they are achieved. Writing out goals clarifies objectives. Being specific makes measuring results simple.

Office meetings can implement goal achievement, if well planned, well run, timely, and lively. A variety of group-dynamics techniques can be used so that meetings will be challenging and interesting to associates. It's a challenge to a manager to come up with 50 bright meeting ideas a year!

Rough times and tough problems call for morale-building sessions. The manager's optimistic attitude when business conditions are poor should be contagious. When tough problems involve team members in an intraoffice squabble, all of the manager's skill in diplomacy will be needed.

We all need a feeling of satisfaction about what we are doing, we like recognition for achievement, and we like opportunities to develop more of our potential.

Review Questions

1. What should objectives be?
2. Why does it help to write goals out and be specific about numbers?
3. List three reasons for having office meetings.
4. Suggest four learning techniques to use in a meeting, in addition to lecturing.

5. Jot down 10 ideas for provocative office meetings.

6. What are major motivators for associates?

7. Name three things a manager can do to tide his or her company over during a recession.

5

Policy and Procedure Manual

Having decided on a company structure, and whether associates are to be independent contractors or employees, the next step is to write a *policy and procedure manual*. This reference guide to a smoothly running company must be understood by all and kept up to date by means of review and revision. Remember the old adage "People support what they create", so share the planning and revision of policies and procedures with all associates.

It may be 15 pages or 150, but cover these basics:

Introduction. This should include a statement of company objectives, its philosophy, a brief history, a description of its organizational structure.

Broker–Associate Relationships, Job Descriptions, and Expectations. Be specific about requirements for associates, such as license, board memberships, auto, and insurance, and about what the company does and does not provide. Include goal setting and evaluation counselling.

Office Procedures. Cover the secretarial and other services available, the records to be kept, who answers the phone, customer rotation and the sharing of office coverage, mailings, housekeeping responsibility, office hours, and the answering service.

Rotation. Your policy on rotation of office prospects is designed so that all associates have equal opportunity to list and sell. For procedure, some offices use a day system, rotating the days, with all new business going to the associate assigned that day. There is usually a "back-up" person. Records should be kept of all prospects, the date they called and/or came in, the source of the prospect, and the results. It is easy to see in a few weeks' time if the system has equalized opportunities.

If associates agree that the office should be covered at all times, their floor time should be fairly shared. We use half-day segments for this time sharing, with associates choosing the morning or afternoon slots that suit their schedules. Both morning and afternoon persons have agreed-on responsibilities that are mutually helpful. For example, the morning associate gets the mail, opens the office, calls the answering service, and may make coffee. The afternoon associate picks up the Multiple Listing Service bulletin and new listings before coming in, and takes the outgoing mail to the post office after closing up the office at night.

The "Caddy" System.   To equalize the number of office prospects that each associate obtains, we use a "Caddy" rotation system in our office. An Oriental tea caddy moves from desk to desk, indicating whose turn it is to take care of the next prospect. Your "caddy" can be any movable object readily visible to all in the office. The names of each associate are listed on a "Caddy" Sheet. When a prospect walks in, telephones, or writes us, the caddy broker is "up". The associate then fills in the name of the prospect, source, date, and results on the caddy sheet. Ideally, the caddy broker will be available, but if not, the next in line should be on hand. If an associate misses a turn while on vacation, a line is drawn to indicate this. At the end of a year, each associate should have received about the same number of office prospects.

When no one is in the office, the caddy person can keep the answering service informed so that someone is always available for evening or Sunday calls.

If neither the caddy broker nor the back-up person is in the office when there is a walk-in, the floor-time person takes the prospect out and counts it as a turn, thus moving ahead on the caddy sheet. If the caddy broker isn't there to answer a phone call about an advertised property, the person who takes the call answers the inquiries, makes an appointment to show the property, and counts that prospect as a turn after the prospect comes in. If it's a "no show", it doesn't count. (See the sample Rotation Sheet in the Appendix.)

An associate's personal referrals do not go on the caddy sheet, which is a record of rotation for prospects generated only by the firm.

P.M.B.O. (Participative Management by Objective).   This suggests that the manager let associates decide on the rotation and coverage system that suits them best. When substitutions are needed, they will arrange it among themselves, trading off vacation time coverage or appointment conflicts.

Listing Procedures.   Cover the importance of listings, how to obtain them, the forms available, and the services offered to clients. Include your company marketing program, the tools available, advertising policies, recommended media, and costs.

Selling Procedures.   Deposits, trustee accounts, receipts or binders, contracts, contingencies, financing, and closings, are covered here, as are suggested follow-up services after the sale for both buyer and seller.

Commission Schedules.   It is important that the apportionment of commissions be spelled out clearly (see the sample page from my manual in the Appendix). Writing out this policy avoids disputes and saves time.

Other Departments.   These include commercial property, rentals, property management, and land subdivision. How do you wish inquiries for these services to be handled? Some firms have a specialist who is qualified to handle such requests. If an associate desires the additional training and acquires expertise in a specialized field, I would turn all inquiries over to that associate. If no one in your firm has the expertise for a specific project, you will, of course, refer the caller to a broker who does.

Referrals.   If you belong to a regional or national referral organization, explain the obligations and procedures. Discuss the advantages of referral business in and out, and suggestions for obtaining and servicing referrals.

Memberships and Education.   What organization does the company belong to? What memberships are recommended to associates? Stress importance of ongoing education and of attending seminars and conventions. Obtaining the designation of GRI (Graduate Realtors Institute®) adds to the professional image of the associate and the firm.

The newest national designation of CRS (Certified Residential Specialist®) takes five years of experience in addition to the completion of courses and other requirements, but it is well worth striving for.

Some firms are willing to pay part of the tuition for certain courses as an incentive for ongoing education, and count this as part of the cost of training.

Drawing Accounts.   Some companies advance a draw, or sum of money, to new employees on a weekly or monthly basis, to be repaid from future commissions. If the employee is unsuccessful in producing listings and sales, the funds advanced may be a total loss. On the other hand, a newcomer may be unable to enter this career field without such financial help. Another option for management is to co-sign a bank loan with the individual to provide funds for the first 90 days.

Independent contractors may not be given drawing accounts, according to Internal Revenue Service. However, the broker may make a loan to an individual as long as a note is drawn up and signed that specifies the rate of interest and the date that the loan is due and payable.

Advancing Funds. Some associates or employees regard their owner–manager as their personal friendly banker, frequently requesting loans or advances on commissions due later. They may be poor money managers or have unrealistic expectations. While the manager would respond to a genuine crisis situation, continual requests for loans or advances should be discouraged.

Buying for Own Account. Does the company expect the usual share of commission when associates buy or sell property for themselves? Does the company expect the usual share of commission when associates buy or sell property for investment purposes? You may wish to encourage investments in real estate with a different commission split on purchases by associates for their own account.

How do you handle the occasional request to be the buyer's agent, not the seller's? (See the sample Buyer Agreement in the Appendix.) Emphasize that all parties to a transaction must be made aware of the client relationship.

Disputes and Legal Fees. Hopefully associates will settle any disputes that may arise among themselves. If a dispute is brought to the manager to settle, the decision of management is final.

No legal action that involves the firm should ever be instituted without management consent. A lawsuit to collect a commission, for example, will be costly in terms of both time and money. Management may agree to undertake legal action upon the advice of an attorney, but your policy manual should clearly state how the costs of the action are to be paid, whether the company wins or loses. These costs are usually shared equally by the firm and the associates.

Termination. The old-fashioned word was "firing" someone. Now it's "career adjustment". Or "career counselling", like "You'd be better off selling stockings than trying to sell real estate."

Termination is one of management's most unpleasant tasks. To make this process least painful to both parties it should be understood at the time an associate joins that the future of the relationship will depend on the associate's being able to achieve his or her written objectives, and that the associate will contribute to maintaining a pleasant office climate and be part of the team. Some managers say, "We'll give you a six-week trial period, and if it looks like we can work well together, we'll review in three to six months."

If you have a problem person in the office, it is only fair to spot it early and give the associate a chance to change. Not all marriages are made in heaven, and terminating the relationship may be healthiest for the company and all the other associates. It may be necessary even when it hurts your pocketbook! Example: A top producer was violating or bending the Code of Ethics and got you in hot water more than once with clients and fellow Realtors®. Surgery is called for; get it done. The company reputation for integrity cannot be measured in dollars.

Clarify at the start of the relationship your termination policies and procedures. Spell out in your guidebook what the associate will and will not be entitled to, what funds are receivable and when they are payable.

If there is a parting of the ways, established procedures that have been understood from the start of the relationship will provide the basis for a businesslike, friendly separation.

When an Associate Leaves. An associate may choose to affiliate with another firm. You may feel hurt, but maintain a pleasant relationship. Promptly sit down with the associate and go over all business pending. He or she receives the appropriate share of any fees for sales already under contract, after the closing of title. Determine who will attend the closing to represent your firm. The buyer should be included in *your* firm's follow-up system, and may be assigned to another associate for this servicing.

Go over all the existing listing contracts of the departing associate. Keep the office copy of the contracts, and assign someone to service the listing and obtain a renewal if the property is not sold by the expiration date. The listing fee may be pro-rated between the original listing agent and the servicing agent, or you may wish to request servicing by the listing person so that he or she can earn the usual share.

Prospect cards should be reviewed and an agreement reached about which are to be followed up by the departing agent and which are to be re-assigned by the manager to other associates. On any sales that later result from prospects followed up by the departing agent, even though then working at another office, your firm should be specified as the selling broker.

Put all of these agreements in writing, and notify the head of the company where the associate will be affiliated. Establish a time limit for your associate's obligation to your firm on the customers and clients handled by the associate after leaving. Six months is usual. Keep the arrangements fair to all three parties: the associate, his or her new firm, and your company.

Don't forget to list all the properties currently rented through the associate; include owner and address, renter and address, date the lease began, date of expiration, amount of rent, amount of security deposit, and date of deposit; provide a copy of the lease.

Under the usual lease agreement, if the renter chooses to purchase the house, the broker's agency will be recognized and the associate paid an agreed upon share. If the renter renews the lease for another year, the associate may receive a share of the commission, although all arrangements are made by the originating office.

If there is a property management contract, clarify who will continue to provide service for the owner.

All supplies furnished by your office should remain there.

Summary

A policy and procedure manual that is understood by all members of the firm is an important management guide. It should be readily available for reference, changed with changing times, and updated periodically — not filed away and forgotten.

As an aid to preparing one, outline your basic policies and the procedures to be followed to implement these policies. One basic policy is that all should share equally in opportunities to service office clients and customers. The procedure that implements this policy is the office rotation system. Another basic policy is that the company should render excellent service to all clients. What procedures have been established to achieve this result?

The time and effort it takes to prepare a policy and procedure manual is a good investment. Every firm is different, so copying some else's manual is not recommended. Let your manual reflect *your* philosophy and *your* way of doing business.

Review Questions

1. Why should your guide to policies and procedures be planned, discussed, and shared by all?

2. What are the advantages of having a written guide?

3. Describe a rotation system that you feel would be fair to all if you were managing an office.

4. Why should a commission-split schedule be included in your guide?

5. How do you feel floor time should be scheduled and shared?

6. Suggest three reasons for terminating an associate.

7. Cite two hypothetical cases in which "the management decision must be final."

8. What are some pros and cons of drawing accounts?

9. Determine what policies you would establish for when an associate leaves.

10. Why is it not a good policy to continually loan money to associates or make advances on commissions due?

6

Training

Over the years I've seen many new licensees with excellent qualifications and potential enter the real estate business, become frustrated after a few months of "spinning their wheels," and leave the industry. Their training program consisted of one sentence: "Here's your desk, here's your phone, lots of luck, you're on your own."

A new person comes into a firm with an enthusiastic attitude. A well-planned and -implemented training program enables the new licensee to acquire the knowledge and skills necessary to be successful.

Why Train?

A strong training program will help achieve the following:

- Attract motivated associates
- Improve communications
- Weed out misfits
- Increase production
- Build company loyalty

For the manager it is worth the time it takes. While a training program cannot be required of independent contractors, they will appreciate the opportunity to participate.

In small offices the training program is too often something the busy manager has little time for. But don't waste Qualified Customer X on brand new Associate Z. Set up a training program, supervise it, inform applicants of it — it's a recruiting tool as well as insurance against lost opportunities for associates in listing and selling.

Who Trains?

The manager may be a skillful trainer but may not have time for the job. You can have a "buddy system" in which an experienced associate with an interest in training takes on the newcomer and supervises the training, taking him or her along on listing presentations and showings. This trainer should be compensated for the job, perhaps with an override of 5 or 10 percent on the new associate's earnings for six months.

Qualifications of a Good Trainer

- **H**as a real desire for the trainee to succeed.
- **O**bservant; notices gestures, facial expressions, posture, tone.
- **P**erceptive; modifies "toughness" and the angle of approach as needed.
- **E**mpathetic; aware of the trainee's "comfort zone" and terminates the exercise at the right time.

This adds up to H-O-P-E. Always thank the trainee for participating. Evaluate each role-play objectively; temper criticism with suggestions for improving techniques. Be compassionate, not critical. The trainee may want to try it with a change of roles; so do that, and you both may benefit. Keep it brief. Afterwards, emphasize the strong points; find out how the trainee feels about the exercise. Relate it to real-life events in your own experience, without getting long-winded. Ask: "Was this helpful? What did you learn?" Point out that it's more *profitable* for them to encounter these situations in the office than to face them unprepared in the field. Be sure that they realize that *most* prospects are much nicer in real life, but it's the ones who aren't that make the training effort pay off.

How to Train

A 40-hour training program may last two hours a day, five days a week, for four weeks—during which time the associate's board application is processed, cards ordered, listing book put together, and office tools and market area learned. Under a training program, the new associate should be in the office every day, learning the routine and systems, and observing experienced associates as they qualify prospects, use the telephone, and handle negotiations. I would not recommend putting trainees on floor time or having them advise sellers or buyers until the training cycle is completed.

Fieldwork should be suggested: learn the territory; see the properties; get to know the records available at the town or city hall; visit schools; meet the builders; walk vacant land; visit bankers; prepare announcement cards;

list friends, relatives, and neighbors they plan to contact; and read—read—read. Read the history of the town, its planning and zoning rules, the board of education reports, and the local paper. Attending town meetings, hearings, etc., is helpful.

It will be a busy month for them, but when it's time to go out on their first listing or selling call, they'll go with confidence and a quiet air of professionalism that comes from knowing what to do and why and how to do it; and they are much more likely to succeed.

A much briefer training program is sufficient for an experienced associate who is changing offices. Orientation to your policies, procedures, forms, and records should be given. Review your training outline with the new associate, and offer assistance with any areas. The experienced person will have a track record of listings and sales that will be helpful in setting goals.

A variety of adult learning techniques can be used in addition to lecturing. Case studies, open-ended questions, and role-playing are effective.

After deciding how much time you are willing to invest in training, write out a program to use. Try it, review the results, and revise the program as needed. The investment will pay off!

Techniques to Try

Training can be fun for the trainer and the trainee. Throwing some unexpected curves into the dialogue livens up the exercise and gives the trainee a taste of what to expect. What Realtor® hasn't had a prospect ask an awkward question? The more imaginative the role-play the trainer designs, the more skills the trainee develops. Basics must be emphasized, but the trainer can tailor the role-play to fit the locality and the prospects that the trainee is most likely to encounter.

To start a role-play, the trainer might walk in with newspaper in hand and say, "I want to see the house with pink shutters." It's up to the trainee to introduce himself, get the prospect's name, and establish the right ambiance for qualifying the buyer. The trainee can throw fast-curve questions and observe the trainee's ability to handle them:

- "I don't have much time. I have other appointments."
- "Just tell me where Red Hill Road is so I can see this For Sale by Owner."
- "Does this house have a basement?"
- "How many high school graduates here go on to college?"
- "Do the kids smoke pot here?"
- "What's the crime rate here?"

- "I really think this town's too far out for commuting."
- "We're just looking, don't have much of a down payment saved up yet."
- "I don't think we can afford the taxes here."

As you exaggerate the difficulties during training sessions, the trainee will become more skillful in interviewing, qualifying prospects, and handling surprises with aplomb, and gain knowledge of what to expect in the field. The trainer will be able to sense whether the trainee will be able to stay in control, or whether he or she will wilt under pressure. Will the trainee take problems personally and become emotionally upset over setbacks? Or will the trainee develop the skills of a professional for dealing with difficult prospects in a profitable, satisfying, equitable manner? The trainer's evaluation of each session should be brief and factual, and repeat specific questions that the trainee could not answer well. Areas of strength and weakness should be noted and discussed with the trainee.

Telephone techniques can be learned through role-plays. The trainer and trainee should not be in sight of each other, and real phones should be used. A useful device for developing a good phone voice is a mirror with "SMILE" pasted on it. Let the trainee *hear* what a difference a smile makes over the phone. A tape recording of the trainee's phone voice may help the trainee develop a warm, friendly telephone personality. (*Note*: Office secretaries benefit from the same training in voice tone, pitch, and tenor.) In a telephone role-play, a trainer must adopt a "tough" role. Prospects sometimes choose telephoning because of the anonymity it affords, and allow themselves to be more difficult over the phone than they would be in person. The caller might refuse to give his name, or might insist upon getting the address of an advertised property so that he can "drive by". The trainee must learn how to get the prospect to divulge his name and phone number, and how to get the prospect into the office to be qualified.

Does the trainee—

- Know the property advertised?
- Have a "switch sheet" on hand?
- Ask for the caller's name and phone number?
- Get and keep control of the conversation?
- Successfully arrange an appointment?

There are books available that discuss fully how to train for listing and selling skills. The same techniques can be used for developing showing and negotiating skills. Remember—your job as trainer is to play a role, and it is okay not to be a nice guy. Act out being *difficult* as a prospect to be qualified, a *critical* looker at properties, a *tough* negotiator trying to get a house for less.

A role-play for negotiating might start with a major price discrepancy between the offer and the listed price—or a minor one. The emphasis should be on the trainee's skill in bringing the two parties into agreement, creating an artful compromise. Does the trainee use all the negotiating tools at hand? Or put too much stress on the same points—the down payment, for instance. Does the trainee have a good understanding of the principles of negotiation? Does he or she give up too easily or tend to side with the buyer more than the seller? What weaknesses need to be worked on?

Keep the session brief—10 minutes or less. Afterward, comment first on all the things the trainee did right, and then share your suggestions for improving the weak responses. Repeat the sessions until both the trainer and trainee feel confident. (See the sample Role-Plays in the Appendix.)

Training Program Outline

I. *ORIENTATION*
   A. *Company Knowledge*
      Background objectives.
      Job descriptions.
      Policies and procedures.
      Forms and tools.
      Records available.
   B. *Board Knowledge*
      Bylaws, MLS, meetings.
      Code of Ethics.
   C. *Market Knowledge*
      Town history, schools, churches, etc.
      Town hall resources and records.
      Town map marked with listings.
   D. *Financing Knowledge*
      Types, banks, and forms.
      Visit several banks, obtain their forms, and practice filling them out.
      Creative financing.

Field work could include the associates' doing a title search of the manager's home. When the associate finds the correct answers for that task, have him search his own title. For example:

TRAINING PROGRAM TITLE SEARCH

I live at _____.
(Address)

I purchased my home on_____.

I paid _____according to revenue stamps.

I had a mortgage of _____ to _____

with terms of _____at_____%.

Are there any tax liens? _____.

Easements?_____. Rights of Way? _____.

My property consists of _____in a _____zone.

A survey is on file, #_____.

The property is shown on Aerial Map #_____.

The tax assessment is_____.

The taxes are _____per year payable _____and _____.

II. *LISTING/SELLING SKILLS*

A. *Listings*
The various kinds of listings, sources of listings, listing contracts, presentation, market comparables, service to client.

Fieldwork may include driving by vacant land listings and builder's houses; check off on map. Complete a market comparable analysis form on one's own house. Prepare one on the manager's house, and practice a listing presentation as if the owner had a "For Sale" sign out.

A valuable tool to help associates obtain listings is a *listing presentation book*. It will take time to prepare, but it is very effective, especially as an aid to beginners. On a first visit to a prospective seller, the book will serve as a guide to ensure a smooth presentation, with no points overlooked. It can be left at the house (where it is sure to be read!) and reclaimed in the evening when the associate returns to the property with a listing agreement to be signed. Something from the book may be left that evening — a company brochure, tips on moving, etc.

Suggestions for a presentation book and some sample pages from ours are included in the Appendix.

B. *Finding and Qualifying Prospects*
   Begin "Gold mine" file of future prospects.
   Plan ongoing contacts.
   Practice qualifying prospects.
   Telephone techniques and switch sheets.
   Ad writing objectives.

C. *Showing Properties*
   Plan the route.
   Know points of interest.
   Know neighborhoods.
   What and how to show.
   Importance of knowing where to find answers to customers' inquiries.

D. *Selling Techniques*
   Trial "closes", signs of interest.
   Obtaining and overcoming objections.
   Knowing when to go back to the seller for additional information.
   Deposits of earnest money, trustee account, binders, contracts.
   Following up on contingencies: termites, building inspection, financing, etc.

E. *Negotiating the Sale*
   Seller vs. buyer interests.
   Seller is your client.
   Obtaining counteroffer.
   Importance of accuracy, of reassurance to both parties, and of followthrough on all contract details.

F. *After the Sale*
   Followthrough for client and customer and emphasis on service.
   Add both to your "contact" file and keep in touch.
   Personal referrals from satisfied sellers and buyers will be a gold mine.

III. *GOAL SETTING FOR SELF*
   Listing and selling production expected.
   Work plan to achieve.
   Listing files completed.
   Prospecting file started.
   Sales tools and materials organized, understood.
   X-Factor sheet completed.

Work Plan

A simple, but effective technique to help an associate get organized is:

PLAN YOUR WORK—WORK YOUR PLAN

Start with a large spiral notebook in which things to do, people to call, and houses to see are all listed. Suggest he attach ads he's called owners on, and jot down phone numbers he may need at home at night. Tick off items finished; bracket or circle "carry over" items, and enter them on the next week's log. (See the sample in the Appendix.) When a notebook is filled up, the associate should keep it! It can be a big help when he makes out income tax returns, especially if he jots down names, places, and what he spent on customers he took to lunch, and if he attaches receipts for gifts he bought. It is excellent substantiation in the event he is ever audited by the IRS, especially if other records or receipts are lost. There's a good feeling of accomplishment as jobs get checked off, and a sense of being well organized and on top of your tasks as you log in:

- What needs to be done?
- What was completed?
- What should be carried over?

Four-Square Plan

Another daily planning device that works well, and that will help the associate get started, is called "the Four-Square Plan for Success". Each day, start with a blank piece of paper divided into four sections, each with four items.

Four Calls	Four Letters
Four Listings	Four New Prospects

List who will be called and who should receive letters, and proceed to detail the plan for the day — then follow through. Although four is a small number of calls to make, four calls *every day* will add up to 1,000 a year. You may want different categories, or a different number. Try it for a week and see what you accomplish.

Suggested calls and letters might be:

Four calls

- to a recent buyer to see if he has any questions;
- to a buyer who hasn't closed yet to check on utility transfer and closing details;
- to a friend who may know someone who is considering moving;
- to a broker in a neighboring town to describe an exciting new listing.

Four letters

- to someone you know, enclosing an article from the local paper that may be of interest;
- to thank someone for sending you a prospect;
- to a former buyer who may be ready to upgrade;
- to congratulate an out-of-town broker whose achievement was described in your monthly Realtor® publication.

Four prospects

- to an out-of-town customer who can't buy now, describing a house of interest;
- to someone who is renting but may want to buy when the lease is up;
- to someone you know who lives near a house just listed;
- to a possible investor — have a property to suggest if he is ready to exchange.

Four listings

- to a client with an activity and market report;
- to a F.S.B.O.;
- to a client whose listing will expire soon;
- to someone whose property meets the needs of a prospect you have, though the house is not on the market.

TABLE 6-1　TRAINEE'S CHECKLIST: AM I READY FOR THE FIELD?

	Yes	No	Maybe
1. Am I familiar with all the office forms?			
2. Do I feel competent in qualifying prospects?			
3. Can I do a good job calling on a "F.S.B.O." ad?			
4. Can I do a convincing listing presentation?			
5. Is is fairly easy to fill out a M.C.V. form?			
6. Do I know where to get the facts I need?			
7. Have I ordered cards and announcements and prepared a mailing list?			
8. Can I handle objections by prospects when showing a house and be skillful in overcoming them?			
9. Do I have a work plan that's workable for me?			
10. Am I familiar with board and MLS policies and procedures?			
11. Am I comfortable with my office policies and procedures?			
12. Have I learned the state licensing laws so that I will never be in violation of one?			
13. Do I have good telephone communication skills?			
14. Will I be ready with a switch sheet if a customer calls on an ad?			
15. Do I feel I can negotiate an offer on a property?			
16. Do I have the patience to hang in there and not get discouraged?			
17. Have I worked out a good "follow up" system?			
18. Do I know all the options for arranging financing?			

A trainee who can answer "YES" to 14 of these is ready to try the field.

Does Training Ever End?

A trainer does not consider the task completed once the agent is out in the field. An associate will encounter unexpected challenges in the work world. Be available for discussion of problems as they arise. In the early weeks of field work, review the associate's work plan weekly and encourage good planning habits. Be alert for items that are missing such as thank you notes, attendance at board meetings, and follow-up calls. After that, quarterly reviews should suffice. The associate's preparations for the review will include making a "scorecard" of accomplishments and strengths and weaknesses, and making comparisons to the associate's previous track record and to the current production of other associates. The trainer or manager can use the review session as an opportunity to get feedback from the associate, and to listen to comments on how the office as a whole is functioning from the associate's point of view. Does the associate feel that the office is living up to its part of their working agreements?

You can't tell all you know in a few weeks of training, but you can cover the basics. For example, to discuss all possible ways to finance a property purchase would take a lot of time and might confuse a new licensee. But the trainer can go over the mortgage forms most commonly used in the area, whether conventional, FHA, or VA. If a problem arises later when a would-be buyer encounters difficulty in obtaining financing, the manager can share his or her knowledge of "balloons", "purchase money mortgages", "second mortgages", "wrap arounds", etc.

In-depth training on a specific subject will be more easily absorbed when a problem comes up. "Necessity Is the Mother of a Willingness to Learn."

Set Yourself Up To Be a Winner!

1. Set realistic goals. (Set no goals that depend on "action by others" because you cannot control the behavior of others.)

2. Have goals that are specific. (x prospects $=$ x clients $=$ x sales $=$ $\$x$)

3. Plan your work—your week—your year. Choose the planning system that fits your style. (Notebook, diary, 3x5 cards, etc.)

4. Reinforce all good work habits by using them daily.

5. Reward yourself.

Efficiency is doing an assigned job the best way.
Effectiveness is choosing which job is to be done first, and doing that well.

Summary

Too often potentially successful licensees are lost to the real estate industry for lack of training. Large firms and franchises have professional trainers to help them avoid this loss. But training is essential to the success of everyone. A new licensee embarking on a career in real estate under the auspices of your firm deserves the opportunity to acquire knowledge and skills through your training program. If such an opportunity is not available, he may feel that he's "spinning his wheels", get discouraged, and go to another firm (one that has a good training program) or change careers.

Training programs should be planned, written down, and revised as needed. The trainer should not only possess knowledge and skills in real estate, but also have an aptitude for teaching and enjoy the challenge.

Subject material should be covered and fieldwork done, sometimes with the trainer accompanying the trainee. Then the new agent can evaluate what he or she has learned. The checklist for trainees evaluates the trainer's effectiveness as a teacher as well as the agent's readiness for real-life experiences.

Review Questions

1. List three reasons for having a good training program.

2. Discuss the qualifications of a good trainer.

3. How can fieldwork during training help a new associate?

4. Suggest three fieldwork projects for a trainee.

5. Discuss three training techniques.

6. Write or act out a training role-play.

7. Design a sample work plan for a week.

8. How long does a training program last?

9. What are the advantages to the trainer of evaluating the trainee's checklist?

10. A good program helps the trainee acquire both knowledge and skills. List three areas of knowledge and four areas of skill that should be covered.

7

Getting Started

Owning your own business requires capital for start-up and maintenance expenses, whether you acquire an existing company, merge with one, or start from scratch. If you consider an acquisition or merger, what are the benefits and the costs? Decisions must be made on location, space arrangements, decorating, furniture, equipment, and supplies.

Analyze your marketing area and observe what the leading firms are doing to remain successful.

Capitalization

A rule of thumb when opening an office is that you must have capital for start-up costs, plus six months of estimated overhead expenses in reserve. Real estate offices have a high failure rate as new business ventures. You can avoid being in the ranks of the failed by employing management expertise and obtaining adequate capitalization to get your firm established.

When you establish your own company, planning to be the owner/broker/manager, you should anticipate future earnings to be as rewarding as your income was before you took on the venture. Profit may not be forthcoming the first year because of the start-up expenses, so be prepared to wait.

A prudent person would expect profit on the dollars and time invested in a new enterprise. It is your own capital, and you are in a high-risk venture. Add 20 percent to the yearly budget for profit, but write off the start-up costs over several years.

In our samples we have:

- Estimated start-up costs of $25,000
- One year's "Plan for Profit" of   72,000
- With a Monthly Budget of   6,000

For opening expenses and six months' reserve capital you need:

- $25,000 + (6 × $6,000) =   **$61,000**

If your personal cash reserves are not adequate, line up resources before you open. Having good credit can keep you going as you become established.

Your area may be less costly. Or more expensive. Work out an appropriate estimate of start-up and maintenance costs for your location and for the size of firm you plan before you risk your capital. (See the sample cost estimate at the end of this chapter.)

Buying an Existing Company

Before starting from scratch, you should consider the option of buying an existing firm. Some owners want to retire; some want to move to a different climate; some wish to pursue another career.

Steps to take when considering the purchase of an existing firm are as follows:

- Obtain figures on income, expenses, and profits for the past three to five years, preferably prepared by a reliable accountant.
- Determine what the tangible assets include.
- List all the assets and liabilities of the firm, including the accounts receivable and the accounts payable.
- Evaluate the intangible assets.
- Reach an agreement with the owner on what a fair multiplying factor would be to arrive at a purchase price.
- Inquire if the owner wishes to sell on an all-cash basis, an installment plan, or a cash-plus-stock plan.
- Compare your investment costs in an established firm with the start-up costs of a brand new firm that could take several years to show a profit.
- Talk to local bankers, attorneys, property owners, competitors to

determine if the company has a good business reputation in the marketing area.

Estimating Value for an Acquisition

A reasonable value for an existing firm can be determined by adding up the tangible assets, the accounts receivable less the accounts payable, a figure for intangible assets and good will, plus the average profits per year times a multiplier factor.

Tangible Assets.   These may include carpeting, desks, chairs, lamps, other furniture and fixtures, office equipment (typewriter, copier, adding machine, etc.), supplies on hand, memberships in a franchise or referral service that can be transferred. The "book value" of these assets has been affected by depreciation figures. Consider the value if they had to be replaced. Check to see if any of the equipment is leased, not owned. Tangible assets also include cash on hand. Accounts receivable are a tangible asset.

Intangible Assets.

- An attractive location with a lease you can assume.
- Excellent associates who will stay under new management.
- An established name and image in the area.
- A good reputation in the business community.
- Established policies and procedures.

Profits Averaged Out.   From gross income received, deduct all expenses, including the owner/manager's salary and taxes. The balance is profit. Make allowances for what profits could be if the owner were not taking a large salary. Substitute the figure that you, as owner, would expect as a salary. Average out the profit figures for three or more years.

A Multiplying Factor.   In a business that carries a large inventory of goods to be sold, such as a hardware, furniture, or liquor store, the multiplier could be 10, 20, or 30 times the average profit figure. In a service business, the multiplier is much lower, usually ranging from 1.5 to 2.0 in the real estate industry. For example, if profits over a 3- to 5-year period averaged $50,000 a year, the value of anticipated profits to be included in the purchase price would be computed as follows:

- If multiplier is 1.5   × $50,000   = $ 75,000
- If multiplier is 1.75   × $50,000   = $ 87,500
- If multiplier is 2.0   × $50,000   = $100,000

Summary of Value.

		Assets	Sale Price
Accounts receivable	=	$27,000	
Less accounts payable	=	5,106	
Net	=	$21,894	$21,894
Tangible assets	=	15,000	15,000
Average profits of $50,000			
x multiplier of 1.75	=		87,500
Intangible assets	=	20,000	20,000
		TOTAL:	$144,394

What Terms Are Agreeable to Seller

For tax reasons, sellers may prefer a stock-purchase agreement or a sale on an installment plan. You may or may not want the present owner to remain on the payroll as a consultant. He may have many valuable contacts that will generate business, and his advice can be helpful during the transition years. If he has been managing a successful firm, you definitely would not want him as a competitor in your market area.

An example of an agreement that might be reached is this: "Seller agrees to serve as a consultant to the company, at a salary of $35,000 a year, for three years. In addition to salary, he will be entitled to company benefits of medical insurance payments and may participate in the company retirement plan. His travel expenses, when necessary to be at the office, will be reimbursed by the company." You would, of course, consult your attorney and tax advisor.

Making a Decision

Having done your research and come up with a price for purchase, you have to compare the cost of acquiring an established firm with the cost of starting a new company. If profits continue, you may be able to recover your initial investment in fewer years than it would take you to realize these profits if you started a new firm.

You will have an opportunity to establish rapport with the seller and the associates. It takes many new businesses five to ten years to recover start-up costs. You may be a quantum leap ahead by purchasing a well-established firm!

Ten Questions to Ask Before Buying an Existing Firm

1. Is it in a desirable location, with adequate parking and favorable lease terms for renewal of space?

2. Is the interior space adequate for your present needs and flexible for growth? If not, and you later find larger space in a good location, can the present lease be terminated easily?

3. How many years will it take you to recover your purchase costs if present profit averages continue?

4. Will the top producers stay, under new management?

5. Is the office attractive? If not, what will it cost to redecorate?

6. Is the current owner willing to be a "consultant" for your firm, on a salaried basis, or does the owner plan to compete in a nearby area?

7. Are the policies and procedures that the associates are familiar with (present rotation system, commission splits, etc.) agreeable to you?

8. Does the company have a good reputation among lending institutions and with creditors?

9. Are files, books, and records in good order so that the information is readily available?

10. Why does owner wish to sell? (Ill health, retirement, moving to another area?)

Location

In looking at available space for purchase or lease, check parking facilities, visibility of your sign, ease of access for customers, and traffic conditions. Corner locations are excellent; ground floor space is by far preferable to second floor space. Negotiate the terms of your lease and whether utilities, repairs, and redecorating are included. If there's room to grow, make it a long-term lease or include an option for renewal because moving can be expensive. The landlord may include a tax escalation clause; when his or her taxes go up, your rent rises in proportion.

Rent and utilities vary. Do you want air conditioning? If the landlord doesn't provide this, add its installation to the improvement costs and increase the utility budget.

Expenses

A key question is this: How much will it cost? Start-up expenses will include:

- Fees to join the local Realtor® board and Multiple Listing Service
- Purchase or lease of office space

TABLE 7-1   SAMPLE STARTING COST ESTIMATE

(For a 4- to 6-person Office)

Month's rent and security deposit for lease	$ 1,000
Electricity (Wiring and security deposit)	200
Telephone (security deposit and installation — 4 phones)	300
License, dues, fees, MLS	500
Decorating, carpeting	3,500
Furnishings	8,000
Equipment, supplies	2,000
Printing, postage — Letterhead, cards	5,000
Brochures	
Maps	
Announcements	
Signs, advertising	1,500
Promotion, give-aways	500
Legal and accounting	1,000
Insurance	800
Secretary	-0-
Cash reserve	700
	$25,000

TABLE 7-2   SAMPLE ONE YEAR'S PROFIT PLAN

	Monthly	Yearly
Rent (including heat)	$ 500	$ 6,000
Electricity	75	900
Telephone (including answering service)	350	4,200
Dues, fees, MLS	100	1,200
Office supplies	100	1,200
Printing, postage	75	900
Advertising	1,000	12,000
Promotion, give-aways	50	600
Insurance	50	600
Maintenance (cleaning, etc.)	100	1,200
Legal and accounting	150	1,800
Secretarial help	400	4,800
Manager's salary	1,000	12,000
Manager's expense (including auto)	500	6,000
Conventions, seminars, training aids	200	2,400
Reserve balance	150	1,800
Returns on investments, taxes	1,200	14,400
	$ 6,000	$ 72,000

- Furnishings, decorating
- Equipment
- Signs, cards, letterhead
- Office supplies
- Advertising, brochures, maps

If you own your own building, you may wish to lease space for the real estate firm and be your own landlord. Keep these accounts separate. Ask your accountant for advice.

Space Arrangement

Whether you choose to take over an existing office or start a new one, you'll consider—

- Arrangement of work areas.
- Choices of appropriate decorating and furniture styles.
- Equipment that will be needed.

In renting, how much space do you need? Plan on a reception area with a secretary's desk, a conference room, the associates' desk area, and a manager's office. While you may start small, with only one or two associates, plan for growth and have desk space for future needs. Include an area for files, supplies, and storage. If there's room, a small refrigerator, a coffee maker, and a water cooler are nice additions. A lavatory is essential.

You have choices in arranging the work areas in your office. Are associates to be in cubicles, with partitions between desks? Or in an open area, usually called a "bull pen"? Cubicles provide more privacy, but they take up space and reduce interaction and communication. Most associates like to know what's going on in listing and sales activity, and feel closer to the action in one big room versus several small rooms.

Do you want prospective sellers or buyers to be interviewed in a reception area, in the conference room, or at the associate's desk? A warm, friendly reception area is preferred by most, rather than trying to squeeze in enough chairs to accommodate a family around a desk. The conference room is usually reserved for occasions requiring privacy, such as submitting an offer, responding to negotiations, or signing papers.

The receptionist–secretary's desk will be up front. The manager should have a small private office so counselling can be held in a quiet setting.

An office layout that has worked well for me is shown on page 70. It was just one big room until we added partitions, closets, and shelves. An architect can help you plan the use of the space you have for maximum effectiveness.

23 ft × 29 ft (667 sq. ft.)

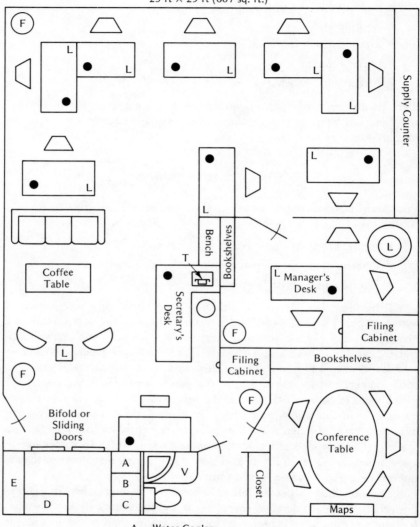

A — Water Cooler
B — Counter Space
C — Refrigerator/Coffeemaker on Top
D — Copy Machine
E — Storage Shelves
F — Plants
L — Lamps
T — Typewriter
V — Vanity
● — Phones

Decor and Equipment

Property improvements (decorating, partitions, rewiring, carpeting, etc.) may be made at your expense or shared by the landlord. Obtain estimates, and have all your agreements in writing to avoid dissension.

Decide on the image of your firm in relation to decor. "Ye olde colonial" or sleek contemporary image? Furnish accordingly. Determine what your capital will provide as you compare brand new furniture and equipment to second-hand shop or tag sale bargains.

Investigate the cost of leasing furnishings and equipment versus buying. Purchasing will have the tax advantage of depreciation but limited capital may indicate leasing. You may be able to get good buys from a company that's going out of business.

Coordinating colors will make the office attractive. Avoid overbright colors and glossy finishes as you choose paint, wallpaper, curtains, and upholstery fabrics. Select materials that are sturdy and require little maintenance. Lots of growing green plants add vitality, but will need some care. Ask the greenhouse salesman for healthy, mini-maintenance plants, so you do not constantly have the expense of replacing them.

In selecting carpeting, remember it's for a business, not a home. A good grade of commercial carpeting will take lots of traffic.

Equipment essentials include an electric typewriter, filing cabinets, and a copy machine. You may do better leasing, not buying, the mechanical equipment if service is difficult to obtain. If equipment is purchased, have servicing contracts. An adding machine, calculator, and postage meter can be helpful.

Graphics

Your company signs, letterhead, business cards, etc., will all have a printing style and color scheme. After you've chosen your company name, consult a graphics expert for advice on a company logo that will convey the image you wish projected. Your printer will help you tie in styles of typeface for printed material and the appropriate color stock for cards and stationery. You may want a brochure about the company, a map of your area, and announcement cards as initial promotion materials. Have a plan; then carry it out with consistency in style and color, and use professional help.

Telephones

When ordering phones, request roll-over numbers and reserve additional numbers for expansion, if available; for example, contract for 5531 and 5532, reserving 5533 and 5534. Connecting your line to an answering service is an extra expense. You may wish to have two or three incoming lines, depending on the size of your staff, and one unlisted number on a call-out line. Stress to associates that one incoming line must be free at all times to avoid loss of business. Their personal calls can be better made from home. Do you want lights on the phones? An intercom button?

Decide how you want to be listed in the Yellow Pages. I found a large ad nonproductive in my area and changed it to a one-inch ad. Our associates like being listed in bold face in the white pages with their business number. Discuss your options with the telephone company representative. Know the cost of this advertising, which will likely be on your monthly phone bill, and measure the results every year before renewing.

Insurance

You will need insurance: a fire/theft policy on office contents, liability insurance for anyone injured on your premises, etc. See what your landlord carries, and then get expert advice from your own agent. Errors and omissions insurance may be available. If you use it, determine if the cost can be shared with associates. A well-trained, knowledgeable, ethical staff *saves law suits* and insurance costs. Ask your insurance agent about the "million dollar protection plan". The premium is quite reasonable because your other policies make up part of the package.

CHECKLIST BEFORE OPENING

		Yes	No
1.	Are there written agreements with team members, either as employees or as independent contractors?		
2.	Are bank accounts (office, trustee) established? Checkbooks on hand?		
3.	Are supplies on hand, including necessary forms?		
4.	Have announcements been sent out?		
5.	Do associates have projects to work on, people to call, notes to send, appointments? Is training completed?		
6.	Has advertising been written and submitted? Have newspapers been ordered?		
7.	If you're going to have an open house, will you serve refreshments?		
8.	If you invited people to drop in "any time" next week, is someone available to welcome them?		
9.	Are arrangements made for cleaning and trash removal?		

You're ready when all nine answers are "YES"!

Celebrate Your Opening

Let the public know that you are open for business. While announcements, advertising, and public relations help, a party is a plus. Allocate some of your promotion and announcement funds for this. Suggest that each associate personally invite friends, neighbors, and former clients, and list the names of those planning to attend. You must know how many are coming.

Refreshments can range from coffee and doughnuts to champagne and quiche, depending on your area, the hours, the season, and the weather. Other ideas of what you might serve include:

- Punch bowl of cranberry juice and ginger ale with open-face sandwiches.
- Wine with cheese trays.
- Mulled cider and snacks (good in the winter).
- Sangria and Mexican dips with chips (good in the summer).
- Iced tea or coffee with cookies or tiny sandwiches.

You might ask each associate to contribute a favorite snack, whether it's a dip, a spread, or a pate.

Be sure that you have acceptances from the guests you expect, and don't assume that everyone who is asked will attend. Large or small, it can be a nice opening party.

Summary

Getting a new business venture established requires capital for both the start-up costs and the monthly expenses until listings are obtained and properties sold. It takes time for a new real estate company to become known and recommended, and the rule of thumb is to have enough cash on hand to cover the expenses for six months.

Writing out cost estimates is one of the first steps. These vary from area to area. Research your option of acquiring an existing firm and compare the cost of acquisition with the cost of starting your own firm.

Consider the potential locations available, estimate the amount of space you need, and plan an office layout. Allow lead time to decorate, furnish, and equip the office, as well as to recruit and train staff. Order signs, supplies, phones, insurance, and other essentials. Prepare opening announcements and advertising.

Review Questions

1. Name two options that you have for owning your own real estate company.

2. Describe how you would estimate the purchase value of an existing firm.

3. How much capital should you have available?

4. What factors will influence your choice of location?

5. List five items on a start-up expense estimate.

6. What bills will need to be paid monthly?

7. How many months does it usually take to reach a break-even point between cash going out and cash coming in?

8. What major purchase items can be depreciated on the books for tax purposes?

8

Essential Records

Keeping good records differentiates the skilled from the unskilled when it comes to managing any business enterprise. The task may be tedious at times, but keeping essential records accurate and up to date is a "must" for managers.

Large corporations have computer control of operations. Market data statistics, track records of each associate, and cost accounting figures are all readily available by pushing buttons. The manager of a small company who is competing with large firms that have the advantage of sophisticated (and expensive) equipment must devise systems that enable him or her to retain control without being buried in paperwork.

Plan a system that works for you. Keep it simple; keep it up.

Master Listing Book

Because listings are your stock in trade, the master listing book should be 100 percent accurate and never leave the office. No listing sheet should be removed until there has been a transfer of title to a new property owner. Then the date of closing, the sales price, and the selling broker are recorded on the sheet. The property address is underlined in *red,* and the sheet is then filed by street address in the SOLD file. This file is a valuable resource for market comparable data. We use looseleaf notebooks indexed alphabetically by streets.

Day Book

A day book, diary, or log on the secretary's or manager's desk records appointments and where associates are. It should include the names of all customers and the source, whether from an ad, a personal referral, a walk-in, or a referral by an out-of-town broker. The day book can be summarized once a week for the activity report so that the manager can see at a glance where new business is coming from, what ads got results, etc. New listings, price changes, transactions, and key information are logged, and each associate checks the day book on arrival.

Phone Log

Phone messages are vital—we use a large message book for this. Who called, for whom, the caller's number, and the time of the call are recorded. As associates get their messages, the entries are checked off. The book is on the desk of the "up" salesperson who answers the phone and takes care of the next seller or buyer. It is that person's responsibility to see that all messages are relayed before the office closes. A reliable phone message system is a must for your business, and the cooperation of all is required because it is to be of benefit to all.

Transaction Book

While associates may wish to have their own files of prospects, listings, and contracts, a central file available to all is helpful. We use a looseleaf notebook, labelled "Transactions". Each associate fills out a transaction record on each sale (see the sample in the Appendix) and adds it to the office notebook. These are kept in chronological order until the end of the year; then they are sorted alphabetically by the name of the buyer. Buyers' names and addresses are typed up and added to the mailing list. The transaction folder for the year is filed.

It's a handy reference if the buyer becomes a seller in a few years because you'll know where the mortgage was placed, the name of the attorney, whether or not there was a termite or building inspection, what was included in the purchase, and other useful information.

Activity Report

A weekly activity report is useful. It summarizes new listings, properties under contract, and titles that closed, and reports all client and customer calls for the week.

Capture Rate

From the weekly activity reports, the manager can measure the results of advertising, know the sources of prospects, and determine the "capture rate" of each associate. For example, one year we found that 14 percent of

ACTIVITY REPORT				WEEK ENDING	
LISTINGS:					
CONTRACTS:					
CLOSINGS:					
CLIENT/CUSTOMER CALLS					
DATE	PERSON	SOURCE	CALL	WENT OUT	ASSOCIATE

our buyers came from ads, 54 percent came from personal referrals, 11 percent were walk-ins, 4 percent came from a national referral service, and 17 percent were sent by cooperating brokers in nearby towns.

"Capture rate" per associate is determined by dividing the total number of prospects by the number of sales for each associate. In our office this consistently averages out to a range of 1 in 4.3 to 1 in 4.8. If the figure becomes 1 in 7 or 1 in 8, it is cause for alarm about that associate. Sales are being lost; what's the problem? While the figure will vary with areas, the steady producers show what can be done.

If associate A has 10 sales after taking out 50 prospects, the capture rate is 1 in 5. If associate B has 5 sales from 50 prospects, the rate is 1 in 10. If A signs up 1 listing out of every 3 presentations to sellers and B signs up 1 in 6, B needs help in listing skills.

Customer Register

In a rolodex or card file on the secretary's desk, keep the names and addresses of prospects. Include phone numbers, the source of the prospect, the date contacted, and the initials of the agent who is working with the prospect. If Mr. Jones calls, saying, "I saw a house last week with someone from your office —", you can easily look up who "someone" was. If an out-of-town broker calls to refer a transferee to the firm, check to make sure that no associate is already working with that potential buyer or seller.

The register helps avoid awkward situations, such as when two associates claim that they contacted a prospect first. If the associate who made the original contact failed to follow through and has been out of touch with the prospect, the manager may decide to assign the prospect to the firm member with the most recent contact.

"Show Slips"

One of our most useful records is a file of "show slips". New houses tend to be "open" listings, not exclusives, and may be shown frequently when the builder is not on the premises. It's routine to immediately send a "show slip" so that the builder knows that we are the agents who brought the property to the buyer's attention. In the event that a prospect contacts the builder directly, which does happen occasionally, the builder has been put on notice that a broker was responsible. We've had several experiences where the builder hoped to avoid a commission by dealing directly with the buyer. In each case, our copy of the "show slip" was convincing evidence to the builder and his attorney, and our fee was paid.

——————————— *Agent's Activity File* ———————————

While an indexed card file for prospects is common on an associate's desk, a second card file is recommended. Categories would include:

- A "tickler" section, with 12 cards for the months, noting on each the anniversaries of closings that call for a congratulations card or a call.
- Auto maintenance and expense record, including mileage, servicing, and registration number.
- Credit cards with numbers.
- Educational courses, dates, places, and costs.
- Expenses, jotted down as they occur, with the dates, names, places, and costs. Especially important are cash disbursements under $25, too easily forgotten.
- Income, with cards giving dates and sources. This should be computed and compared with the W-2 form sent annually to the IRS by the firm.
- Insurance, including a list of policies carried and the premium due dates.
- Listings with dates, sources, listing prices, sales prices, and days on the market.
- Mailing list with names and addresses.
- Memberships, dates joined, and dues paid.
- Rentals, with names, addresses, and phone numbers of tenants; dates that leases expire; rents; security deposits; and names, addresses, and phone numbers of owners. Cross-reference this to the "tickler" file by the month that the show clause begins.

——————————— *Ad Call Costs* ———————————

In planning your recordkeeping systems, keep them simple, with a minimum of paperwork for associates. You want them in the field, where "S.T.P." (See The People) is what pays off, not paperwork.

I've heard managers complain, "All that paperwork wastes a lot of time." Your system should save time, not waste it. But whatever is worth doing is worth measuring, and good records are the hallmark of a well-run firm. For example, divide your total classified advertising cost by the number of calls you received in answer to these ads. This determines how many dollars it takes to make the phone ring. Is your cost $15 per call or $50? What percentage of callers comes for appointments? What percentage buys? It's a means by which to measure the effectiveness of your advertising program.

Sample Letters

One timesaver in our office is a sample letter file. Included are letters to —

- Out-of-town prospects, enclosing information about our community, a company brochure, and our "care kit".
- Clients, with a copy of the ad that we ran on their property.
- Referring brokers, acknowledging a prospect and confirming our agreement on a cooperative sale.
- Prospects, thanking them for the opportunity to show them properties.
- New neighbors, introducing a buyer (with the buyer's permission, of course) who will soon be moving in.

Whether the typing is done by a secretary or an associate, samples save time. We have a worksheet for appraisals, from which it's easy to type a narrative report (see the sample in the Appendix).

Mailing Lists

Mailing lists are important, whether for direct mail, seasonal greetings, or announcements. Your list should include attorneys, bankers, builders, corporation personnel directors, community organization leaders, and cooperating brokers, as well as the sellers and buyers you've worked with.

If you plan on direct mail promotion, type the mailing list on labels that can be copied to save future addressing time. Keep your mailing list up to date.

Follow Up

A "tickler" file is important in keeping track of listing expiration dates, lease renewal dates, buyer follow-up on anniversaries of purchase, etc. A simple system for a tickler file uses 3 × 5″ cards in a file box on the manager's desk. Each month dates can be checked over and the follow-up jobs assigned. A sample card might be:

```
APRIL

    Y. R. Kerrigan - 24 Elm Street
    our listing, on a 2 yr lease unfurnished
    $500/mo rented by J. G. 6/15/79 to 6/15/81

    $500 security deposit in trustee acct.

    4/15/81 -- show clause starts

    Contact Owner:  John Kerrigan
                    NYC (212)964-2275

    Contact Tenant:  Charles Simpson
                     853-2458
```

A follow-up program during the transition phase of a sale and one for after the sale should be planned and implemented. Going that extra step to help both the seller and the buyer during the transition stage between the contract of the sale and the actual closing is important. It can earn a lot of goodwill for the associate and for the firm. It will result in personal referrals of sellers and buyers, a great asset for future listings and sales.

Some agents may feel that once contracts are signed, there's nothing more that need be done until it's time to get the check at the closing. Some may be too busy to do a good follow-up job; others lack the skill in attention to details. Management's task is to supervise the follow-up procedures.

During training, company policies for follow-up may have been covered by the trainer, but they may have meant little to an associate who is brand new to the field. When that associate has a first sale, the manager should review the follow-up process and clarify what records must be kept in the office transaction file. Those include:

- Copy of listing
- Copy of binder
- Copy of contract
- Copy of mortgage commitment
- Copy of tax bills
- Fuel adjustment report
- Building inspection report
- Termite inspection report

- Any bills paid by the office for care of the property when vacant

Some of the detail work can be handled by the secretary.

Until an associate has developed skill in following up, guidance by the manager is essential. This job can be simplified by using a checklist.

An associate's follow-up doesn't stop on the day of the closing. He or she may take the sellers out to lunch and write them a nice thank you letter at their new address. They'll be writing their old friends in your community, and the words of praise for the service you rendered help your business. Gifts to buyers are another form of follow-up and may be included as part of your public relations program.

CHECKLIST FOR TRANSACTION

	Date Done	By
Contracts:		
Security deposit in trustee account		
Contracts drawn		
Contracts signed by seller		
Contingencies:		
Building inspection		
Termite inspection		
Financing		
Other		
Subagents notified		
Lock box removed		
Pre-Closing:		
Telephone application		
Electric service transfer		
Heating fuel agreement		
Insurance arranged		
Change of address cards sent		
Obtain new address of seller		
Day of closing:		
Property inspection by buyer		
Keys collected to turn over to buyer		
Invoice for fee prepared for seller		
Warranties obtained from seller		
Appropriate letters sent		
Call on new owners		

Summary

Control is the key word for recordkeeping. Records provide a management tool for a smooth-running office and keep valuable data easily available.

Before instituting a recordkeeping system, answer the following questions:

- What is the objective?
- Is this the best way to achieve it?
- How much time will it take?
- Who will give the time?
- What responsibilities go to others, and are they willing to do the job?
- How will we use these records to make our company more successful?

Perhaps you'll hear or read about a system that works well for another Realtor®. If you feel it would be helpful in your office, try it. If it works, keep it. If not, discard it.

Review Questions

1. List five types of records essential in a real estate office.
2. How is "capture rate" determined? Why does a manager need to know this for each agent?
3. Suggest five categories for sample letter forms.
4. What are the advantages of a good follow-up system?
5. Name five items to include in an agent's transaction file.
6. Describe an agent's activity card file.

9

Bookkeeping
and
Budget

_____ **_Venture Capital_** _____

Funk and Wagnalls International Dictionary (1978) defines _entrepreneur_ as "A person who organizes and manages any enterprise, especially a business, _usually with considerable initiative and risk_" (italics added).

Your venture capital is risked, in anticipation of future profits. Your initiative and leadership qualities will be supported by good organization systems. Estimates of the percentage of new business ventures that fail vary from source to source. Figures cited range from a 50% to 80% failure rate.

Contributing factors include the following:

* Not having management expertise
* Underestimating start-up costs
* Not being realistic about how many months it will take to generate income and have a positive cash flow
* Not having sufficient capital (or the ability to obtain financing) to keep going until there _is_ a positive cash flow
* Neglecting to have a "plan for profit" written budget as a guide
* Not maintaining adequate cost controls of day-to-day expenditures
* Failing to keep good bookkeeping records
* Failing to be aware of trends and conditions and planning accordingly.

Some basic understanding of bookkeeping and budgeting will help you succeed.

_____ *Bank Accounts* _____

The company needs a checking account and a separate trustee bank account because the law requires that you never co-mingle the funds of others with your own funds. If your state licensing laws require that interest be paid on security deposits or escrow funds, establish either a savings account for those or a combination savings–checking account on which interest is paid on the average daily balance.

_____ *Bookkeeping Records* _____

Get professional help to set up your books so that all the essential information will be readily available for the preparation of tax returns. This also provides you with a true picture of your financial condition every month.

Your bookkeeping records will include:

- *Cash Receipts Journal* which will show all income of whatever nature, with the exception of that received for the trustee or escrow account.
- *Check Register* which will be a transcript of your checkbook, showing all outgoing monies. (A *Petty Cash* fund may be maintained to cover miscellaneous cash payouts such as postage due, certified mail, or other expenses too small for a check. This fund will be reimbursed as required, showing expenses covered on the stub of your reimbursing check.)
- *Cash Receipts Record* which will show the sources of income (listing, sale, appraisal, rental, property management, etc.)
- *Cash Disbursements Record* which will show the nature of disbursements (appropriate columns include rent, telephone, advertising, office expenses, salaries, commissions, etc.)
- *General Ledger* which will be a monthly summary of the totalled columns that have been posted and balanced.
- *Bank Reconciliation* which will be done monthly when your statement is received from the bank. Check deposits to see that they agree with your records. Tick off checks that have cleared. Any outstanding checks are listed and the total of these, plus your checkbook balance, will equal the balance shown on the bank statement.

Sample ledger sheets that will be a guide for setting up your books are shown in the Appendix.

Budget — Cash Flow

Forecast anticipated earnings and establish a budget. Some expenses, like rent, are fixed. Some, such as advertising, are variable. Gradually you will be able to chart high income months and low income months, and budget accordingly. For example, if November and December are traditionally low income months in your area, you can reduce your advertising expenditures for those months. In southern areas, these might be your best months for advertising expenditures.

Cost Controls

The budget cannot be planned, filed away, and forgotten. Compare planned expenditures and actual expenses every month. Note whether these are plus or minus and to what degree. Keeping track of these figures will be a big help when you write next year's budget. Set up on a quarterly basis. See pages 88 and 89 for a sample.

Desk Cost

The budget for expenses determines the cost for each associate, called _desk cost_. If the budget calls for $60,000 in expenses for the year and there are four associates, the desk cost per associate is $15,000.

If on a 50/50 split, the associate takes home $15,000 from the listing and selling fees and the company retains $15,000 for overhead expenses. Overhead expenses include the manager's compensation.

To determine desk cost, divide the number of active associates into the expense figure. Do not count the secretary's desk, the manager's desk or an empty desk. For example:

$$\frac{\$60,000 \text{ in expenses}}{4 \text{ associates}} = \$15,000 \text{ desk cost per associate}$$

Commission Splits

Why is it important to know desk costs? It's a means to measure the effectiveness of each associate. If the projected cost is $15,000 and associate A earns $15,000, the profit percentage is zero on associate A's desk. If B earns $22,500, the profit percentage is 50 percent on that desk. If C earns only $7,500, there's a loss of 50 percent.

COST CONTROLS
1st Quarter

ITEM	Annual Budget	January Actual	February Actual	March Actual	TOTAL for Qrtr	Remaining in Budget
Rent	6600 -	550 -	550 -	550 -	1650	4950 -
Heat	1800 -	200 -	180 -	160 -	540	1260
Utilities	720.	75 -	70 -	70 -	215.	505
Telephone	6000.	525	550	600	1675	4325
Answering Service	360	30	30	30	90	270
Repairs & Mainten	1200	45	65	112	222	978
Office Supplies	1200	72	44	30	146	1054
Postage	540	—	90	12.50	102.50	457.50
Insurance	600	—	280 -	—	280 -	320
Legal & Accounting	2400	300 -	—	—	300	2100
Taxes	600 -	—	200	—	200	400
MLS	900	—	300 -	—	300	600
Licenses, Member- ship & Fees	400	190	—	20 -	210	190
Travel & Education	3000	—	—	540 -	540	2460
Auto Expense	1200	90	75	120	285	915
Advertising --						
Newspaper	24,000	900 -	1125.	1,850 -	3,875 -	20,825
Institutional	1,000	120	80	—	200	800
Brochures	1500	—	500 -	—	500	1,000
Directory	300	120	—	—	120	180
Photos - Other	300	—	85 -	—	85	215
Public Relations	600	45	—	85	130	470
Entertainment	600	—	60 -	40	100	500
Gifts	1200	60	75	40	175	1025
Contributions	300	—	40	25	65	235
Furniture & Equipment	900	225	—	80	305	595
Miscellaneous	600	40	20	55	115	475
Salaries --						
Manager	15,000	1250	1250	1250	3750	11,250
Secretary	7500	625	625	625	1875	5625
Bookkeeper	2400	200	200	200	600	1800 -

	April Actual	May Actual	June Actual	TOTAL for 6 Months	Remaining in Budget			
1								
2								
3								
4								
5								
6								
7								
8								
9								
10								
11								
12								
13								
14								
15								
16								
17								
18								
19								
20								
21								
22								
23								
24								
25								
26								
27								
28								
29								
30								
31								
32								
33								
34								
35								
36								
37								
38								
39								
40								

89

Some firms have variable commission splits where the percentage of commission paid to agents increases after a base desk cost is reached. For example, if the desk cost is $15,000, all net commissions up to a total of $30,000 will be split 50/50. After an agent has earned $15,000 in take-home fees, commissions may be split 55/45 or 60/40, the larger share going to the associate. It's an incentive plan that helps to retain good producers by increasing the rewards of their efforts.

_____ *Company Dollar* _____

Let's look at the *company dollar* concept. The gross dollar (all income received) might look like this:

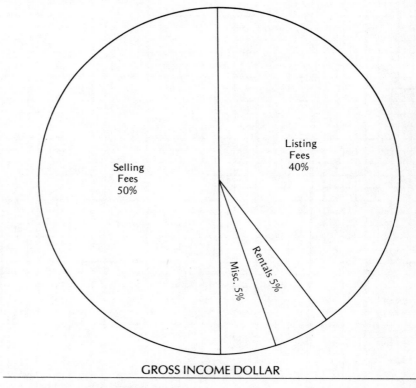

GROSS INCOME DOLLAR

50% from commissions on sales
40% from commissions on listings
5% from commissions on rentals
5% from miscellaneous (including property management, appraisals, _____etc.)
100% total

From this gross income, deduct payouts to listing brokers, referring brokers, and selling brokers. What's left is the *company dollar*, the basis of your budget, because you can control what is spent.

Gross company dollar is the amount left after all out-of-office commissions have been paid out before associates in the office are paid. *Net company dollar* is the amount left after both out-of-office and in-office commission fees have been paid.

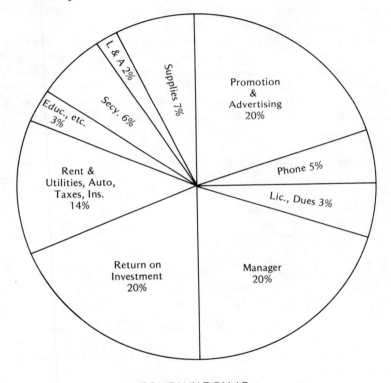

COMPANY DOLLAR

Company dollar was budgeted:

20% advertising and promotion
5% phone, answering service
3% license, dues, fees
14% rent, utilities, taxes, insurance
2% legal and accounting fees
6% secretary
7% supplies, equipment, depreciation
3% education, conventions
20% manager's compensation
20% return on investment

The Bottom Line

The key item in your list is the bottom line, or what is left as profit after expenses are met. Your budget should plan for profit. If you are both the owner and the manager, you are compensated for managerial time. To estimate this figure, what would you be worth to another company?

You don't need to be an accountant to figure out where the money comes from and where it goes. You need to be a good manager to keep a healthy bottom line with an eye on where the dollars go and why.

National surveys suggest some parameters for percentages of expenditures, but this varies with areas. In your marketing area, 10 percent of the company dollar spent on advertising may be enough. In other areas it may be 20 percent or more to keep up with competition. In your first year of business, the promotion figure may be higher, as you strive for recognition, and there may be no profit. As you become better established, building a productive team, the percentage of profit in the company dollar will increase.

Recent research shows that on a nationwide basis, the average percentages are:

16–18%	Advertising and P.R.
10–15%	Salaries (secretary, bookkeeper, plus legal and accounting fees)
10–15%	Supplies, auto, etc.
7–10%	Occupancy
5–9%	Telephone
7–10%	Manager's salary
24–41%	Return on investment

Options to Increase Profits

Some of the options you have to increase the bottom line figure are as follows:

- Add more associates (without getting beyond your span of control).
- Reduce expenses (without eliminating essentials).
- Increase productivity in listings and sales for all associates by training.
- Replace the poorest producers.

Review expenses monthly, and compare the percentages with your estimates.

Some firms have changed their company structure from that of associates being independent contractors to that of an employer–employee relationship. With higher company expenses for Social Security payments and bookkeeping help, management may decide to change the commission split arrangement from 50/50 to 53 percent for the company and 47 percent for the employee. Some company budgets are based on a 60/40 commission split basis, 60 percent to the company. What will attract good associates in your area and still produce annual profits?

Summary

A good bookkeeping system is essential to any business enterprise. Systems vary according to market areas and the volume of business. (See the sample ledger sheets for a typical small residential office in the Appendix.)

An annual budget should be planned and revised as needed. A simple cost control system helps the manager compare projected expenditures with actual expenses. The budget will determine the "desk cost" figure. Control of the company dollar — the net to the firm, not the gross income received — determines what percentage will remain as profit: the "bottom line".

Review Questions

1. Define *venture capital*.
2. List five factors that may cause a new real estate firm to fail.
3. What should bookkeeping records include?
4. How is *desk cost* determined?
5. Define *company dollar*.
6. Suggest three options a manager has to increase profits.

10

Secretarial and Other Services

_____ *Secretarial Services* _____

Time Value

In opening or expanding an office, you may wish to have a part-time or full-time secretary. To help you decide when this is practical, know what your time is worth. If you estimate that you work 50 hours a week for 50 weeks to earn $25,000 as a salesperson or manager, your time is worth $10 an hour. You can free up your time for listing, selling, and management by engaging secretarial help that is available for less per hour. If used part time — 9:00 A.M. to 1:00 P.M. for example, five days a week — it's not too costly and can increase your effectiveness.

Keep track of how many hours you spend keeping books, filling in the ledger columns, writing checks, and balancing the bank statement. If it is 20 hours per month and you can engage a bookkeeper for $6 to $8 an hour, decide if you can use your time more productively elsewhere.

Interviewing

If you plan to have a secretary, a blind ad in a newspaper ("send resume to Box X") should bring good response. I had 40 replies to one ad, selected six of the best written letters and resumes, and set up appointments for personal interviews. At the interviews, the job description was discussed, references requested, and personalities appraised. In our office the secretary is also the receptionist — the first person a customer sees, so appearance is important. The voice that answers your telephone should be pleasant.

A smile, manners, warmth, and neatness all count. She is, in effect, your official hostess whose graciousness welcomes visitors and makes them feel important. Some applicants may be overqualified and wince when they hear that their job includes making coffee, emptying wastebaskets, washing ashtrays, etc. But jobs are only demeaning when so regarded by the individual. Hopefully, the secretary will take pride in being part of a productive office.

Some applicants may wish to use the secretarial job to get experience for becoming a salesperson or broker. This may suit your long-range goals or it may not, but discuss the possibility openly. Some may say, "No, I'd never want to work weekends or evenings."

Review your office policy for holidays, vacations, and sick leave and any company benefits.

Good typing skills are essential; shorthand is an asset. You might ask an applicant to type a sample letter and observe how long it takes. Accuracy, neatness, and speed can be evaluated. Inquire into bookkeeping experience. You will have judged their telephone skills and voice quality from your call to arrange the interview.

Describe their tasks and your expectations clearly. Tell them you are interviewing others. Call all back to thank them with a polite explanation like "I chose someone with more experience in our kind of work." Check out references for your choice.

Training

Next, train the secretary in —

- Answering the telephone.
- Keeping the log and message book.
- Maintaining the master listing book.
- Using office equipment, maintenance.
- Your filing system.
- Sorting incoming mail.
- Receptionist duties.
- Updating the customer register.
- Inventory and re-order of supplies.
- Responsibility for relaying messages.
- Preparing weekly activity report.
- Routine tasks, like clipping ads and mailing them to clients with a covering letter, sending out brochures and letters to out-of-town requests, and writing thank you letters.
- Maintaining a "tickler" file, alerting associates to expiration dates on listings and rentals.

- Keeping records of available listings, who sold what, how our company compares with competing firms in terms of numbers of listings and sales.
- Odd jobs — running errands like picking up keys, material from printers, information from the town hall, getting sandwiches, etc.

Be sure that you establish an agreement that the secretary works for you, and while helpful to all in the office, task priority is for the manager. If she's overrun with requests from associates ("make these appointments", "cancel these appointments", "get out these letters"), you must step in and clarify to the associates what are reasonable and unreasonable demands on her time.

You may reach a stage where company needs dictate two part-time secretaries, or one full-time secretary. It's added expense, so evaluate what is being done, what needs doing, and who can do it best.

A good secretary saves management time, acting as a buffer for interruptions, screening out long-winded equipment or encyclopedia salespersons and fund solicitors, and opening and sorting mail into "to read", "to answer", "to pay", etc., folders. The secretary should have the ability to establish priorities on paperwork, meetings, correspondence, and special projects, reminding the manager of priorities as needed. Keeping good files so that items can be located quickly is essential.

Your "gal Friday" can be the cornerstone of office effectiveness, and can double the productivity of the staff with her skills in time and project management.

Telephone Techniques

Your telephone is crucial to your business and should be answered 24 hours a day. This can be done by a human answering service or by machine. I prefer an intelligent answering service that can immediately contact the manager or an associate when there is no one in the office. A prospect who calls on an ad usually wants an immediate response and may hang up on a machine. Answering service personnel are trained to obtain the caller's name and number.

How the telephone is answered is also important. Whether you are in the office or out, good fielding of your calls is essential. In our office we identify the firm and the individual who answers the phone: "Dorothy Bates Real Estate, Mary Smith speaking." Many firms use "Good morning, ABC Realty" or "Good afternoon, XYZ Real Estate", but I feel that identification of the person who answers is more important than informing the caller whether it is AM or Pip Emma!

You expect the callers to give their names, so start by giving them yours. Telephone skills are essential and part of your training program for all office personnel.

Suppose you are in a counselling session and have asked to have calls withheld unless important. The smart colleague will cooperate by getting the caller's name and promising a call-back within the hour or, if in her opinion it is important, by bringing in a memo with "London banker, line 2, Mr. Wells-Stratton". And, with an apology to your conferee, you can take the call.

When you're out of the office, your staff member may answer with, "He's not in. May I ask who's calling?" or, more effectively:

- "He's teaching a course on Ethics today, but he can call you after 5 PM. May I have your number, please?"

- "She's at an educational seminar now. May she call you this evening?"

- He's out of town at a national Realtors® meeting, but I can reach him this evening. If it's important, he can call back before Monday."

Never, never use "He's not in. Want to leave your number?" Or "Don't know where she is. Want to try her at home?"

Associates can benefit, too, from training in telephone techniques. It's much more image building to say, "He's out inspecting properties, but can call you at 2 PM." Or "She's at the bank arranging a mortgage for someone. Please give me your phone number."

The way your phone calls are handled creates an image for the firm; keep it a professional one.

Callers are likely to respond favorably to "She had an appointment, but I expect her in by 11 AM and she can call you then — or if it's urgent, I'll try to reach her." Versus, "She's at the beauty parlor."

Every member of the team helps each other in handling phone calls, as well as in keeping track in the message log.

As manager, listen to the responses you hear when the phone rings in your office. Are the responses image builders for the company and the associates? If not, it's time for an office meeting that could be billed as "The Instrument and The Image", a skill-sharpening session on fielding phone calls. Use some case histories, but with no names.

Introductory remarks: "You're all up for batting practice here, though some have a high average already." Pose problems for them to solve. For example:

CALLER:"Mr. Williams, please."

ANSWERER: "He's not in. May I have your name?"

CALLER: "When do you expect him?"

ANSWERER: "Don't know. Want to try him at home?"

Ask them to suggest better answers to the two questions.

Questions to Ask Before You Hire a Secretary

1. What do I expect her to do every day?

2. Will I give the necessary time to train her for her responsibilities?

3. What are her expectations from the job? (Is it a steppingstone to becoming a sales associate? If so, discuss this frankly.)

4. Is she a good organizer? Does she enjoy details?

5. Does she have a pleasant telephone voice? (And will she be diligent about recording and referring all messages?)

6. If her duties include being a receptionist, does she have a warm welcoming personality?

7. How does she feel about keeping the office neat, making coffee, taking out the trash, going on errands for supplies, to the post office, etc.?

8. What company benefits does she expect, in addition to salary?

9. Is she aware that her number one loyalty is to the firm, and to the manager's need for assistance?

10. Will I feel comfortable working with her?

Examples of Daily Tasks for a Secretary

1. Open and sort the mail, dividing it into the following categories:
   - Bills to pay
   - Letters to answer
   - Requests for donations
   - Things to read
   - Property brochures
   - Junk mail
   - Personal letters (not to be opened)

2. Bring the master listing book and prospect registers up to date.

3. Type office letters, leases, reports, appraisals, etc.

4. Keep an inventory of office supplies and replace them as needed.

5. Check the tickler file.

6. Keep a file of "Solds" by street address with title-passed price — valuable information for future appraisals or listings.

7. Answer the phone, and record and convey all messages.

8. Help in maintaining the appearance of the office, which may include emptying ash trays, wastebaskets, and coffee cups; watering plants; replacing desk blotters; vacuuming; etc.

9. Save management time by screening people requesting donations or selling something.

10. Greet people who come to the office, and get them coffee if they'd like it; help associates make appointments if needed.

Ten Reasons Secretaries May Be Fired
(As Cited by Various Brokers)

1. Incompetent work: poor typing skills, inability to keep files organized, lack of attention to details, errors in letters and forms.

2. Too much time wasted on chit-chat in the office; too many personal phone calls.

3. Unable to establish priorities and adhere to a "first things first" routine.

4. Became "too friendly" with one associate and began to steer all prospect calls that way instead of following the rotation procedures.

5. Treated associates and/or customers in an officious manner.

6. Was careless about telephone calls; failed to refer and record messages.

7. Was not interested in the office's appearance; allowed dirty coffee cups and ash trays to sit around too long after busy sales personnel rushed off to appointments.

8. Frequently late to work; too many requests for time off.

9. Not really interested in the growth and prosperity of the firm.

10. Talked too much outside the office instead of keeping information on offers, etc., confidential.

Business Machine Technology

We live in an age of computer technology and you may choose to take advantage of it.

Business systems machines are available that can save hours of manual labor in handling paperwork. By creating a professional image, an appropriate machine could give your firm a decided edge over the competition in your marketing area.

A sample system could consist of four main parts:

1. An electric typewriter to use in recording data, with keys for retrieving material.

2. Tapes or discs for storage of data.

3. A display screen, similar to a small TV, on which you can view or revise material before printing.

4. A machine that types perfect letters, reports, envelopes, labels, and promotional material in very few minutes. The data printed can be on your letterhead or other paper.

All entries are coded by number and can be recalled by pressing a few buttons. The operator's notebook records the key numbers.

Following are some examples of files that may be stored:

- Prospect list, with name, address, source, date contacted, price range, and associate assigned
- Listing file, with owner's name, address, price, size, style, date of expiration, listing broker, commission, etc.
- Transaction records
- Sample letters and reports
- Market comparable data
- Rental file
- Sales tracking file

Examples of Use. For each new listing, get a printout of the prospects who may be interested; ask the machine to type letters to these prospects requesting an appointment to show. A paragraph describing the new listing can be typed once and inserted in your form letter.

Your operator can punch the key for expiration dates within a time frame on your listings and have the machine type the letters asking for a renewal. A paragraph can be inserted describing current market conditions and a forecast for future activity.

Market comparable data are available in seconds when you need to obtain an exclusive listing that's priced right or to write an appraisal report.

A list of available rental properties should be on file, coded for furnished or unfurnished, style, number of rooms, price, etc. When rented, add the expiration date of the lease to the file so that you can be in contact with the property owner, listing broker, or tenant, whichever is appropriate, when the "show" clause goes into effect.

Machines may have variable type styles and sizes, and are usually available on a lease or lease–purchase arrangement.

A key question, in addition to the initial cost, is: Who will be trained to program and operate the system? It requires skill, and you would not want to lose the only person in the office who can use it if you make the investment in the equipment and the training of the operator.

_____ *Bookkeeping Services* _____

Your trustee account must be kept impeccably to retain your license. You can do it yourself or turn it over to a bookkeeper. You may start out doing all jobs yourself, but as you grow, delegate time-consuming tasks to qualified personnel.

On a low cash-in–cash-out basis (for example, 3 to 5 commission checks received each month, 10 to 20 checks out), a quarterly reconciliation of accounts may be all you need. When 15 to 20 checks come in each month and 80 to 100 go out, monthly bookkeeping help will be a big time-saver.

The bookkeeper can also prepare your tax returns, or you may decide to use a CPA.

A cash flow statement will be helpful in reviewing and revising your budget. The information is gathered from transaction sheets, but remember that not all sales close.

You may also wish to train a secretary or bookkeeper to take over some of your recordkeeping tasks, such as prospect sources and advertising results.

_____ *Cleaning Services* _____

In the early days of a company, when the budget is very limited, the manager may be running the vacuum cleaner at night, washing windows, and dusting the furniture.

These jobs can be done by a cleaning service on a daily or weekly basis. Inquire into costs, select a reliable service, and budget the item. Your time and that of your staff can be used more creatively in other areas.

Arrangements must be made for trash removal; find out the pickup days and costs, and allocate the jobs of emptying wastebaskets and having trash bags ready for pickup.

Summary

Secretarial services can be a great administrative aid, giving a manager more time for creative planning, cost controls, recordkeeping, and counselling. Job requirements should be discussed and the necessary time taken to train a secretary. Good telephone techniques are as important as typing skills.

Office business machines are available that can file and retrieve data, provide instant updates, and duplicate perfect letters, among other things. A trained operator is needed. The cost necessary to buy and maintain this sophisticated equipment must be weighed against the time value of the hand labor saved.

A bookkeeper is skilled in reconciling bank statements, posting ledgers, preparing cash flow statements, paying bills, and preparing required IRS forms. Because these are all time-consuming tasks, and because records must be accurately maintained, professional help is worth the expense to most managers.

Review Questions

1. List five qualities that you would look for in a secretary.
2. Write a job description for a secretary.
3. List 10 routine tasks that a secretary can do.
4. Give five causes for firing a secretary.
5. Discuss what a business systems machine could do for a real estate firm.
6. List five tasks that a bookkeeper could do for you.

11

Time Management and Delegating

Time is the great equalizer — we all have the same amount of it. How effectively we use time separates winners from losers. Ben Franklin said, "Time is money — Spend it wisely." Your management of time will depend on —

- Your ability to set priorities.
- Your self-discipline to do "first things first".
- Your willingness to delegate tasks to others.

Priorities

To establish priorities, get in the habit of writing everything down, both business and personal, that demands your time.

Choose a time organization system that suits you — a pocket diary, a small looseleaf notebook, a day book, or 3 × 5 cards — but have a system! Include commitments to family and community as well as business. Decide each day on priorities, and number the items on your list in order of importance. Do the number one job first, then go on to two. Problems will arise and all the items on the list may not be ticked off by the end of the day; add those to your list for tomorrow and again decide on priorities.

Usually, when we label the job we least like doing number one, and get it out of the way first, we'll find a surge of energy for other tasks. The job we were reluctant to tackle (such as confronting someone in what could become an unpleasant 30 minutes) may drag on our subconscious all day and use up valuable psychic energy. Do it first, get it over with, and go on to other projects.

The satisfaction of getting things done is an energy-charger. Don't even open your mail until you've ticked off Item One on your list!

Postponement of important tasks is rarely productive, but you may acquire some extra time when low priority problems solve themselves, so set these aside.

Set an example for associates on organizing time—and help them manage theirs better. Share your system, but encourage them to establish one that works for them. How they use their time is a major factor for reaching their objectives.

Expect the unexpected, anticipate interruptions, and be flexible—but adhere to priorities. When the crisis is over, go back to number one. Keep visible what needs doing. Sometimes what appears to be a crisis may be set on a back burner, to boil over or not, but a limited response may be effective. The situation may resolve itself with no action by you.

Group similar tasks together—e.g., recordkeeping, advertising, letter answering. Consolidation of like tasks is a time-saver.

Cluster your phone calls, making a list and allocating only the essential time for each. Clarify your objective before you dial, achieve it, exchange pleasantries, and terminate your call.

Time Stealers

We all encounter them; treat them the way you would a robber of your silverware! Your in-basket, full of junk mail, is one. Solicitors for magazines, charities, and new products are another. As are associates who want to give you a word-for-word report of their three-hour encounter with a seller or buyer, and long-winded telephoners—be they friends, clients, or customers—who want to bend your ear "if you're not busy".

How do we deal with these time stealers? What bright thoughts and creative enterprise are they robbing you of?

Recognize the worth of your time, your attentiveness, your energy, and your creativity, and learn to be pleasant but brief.

Time Savers

Most of us are creatures of habit, and to change these habits takes effort. If you want to manage your time better, start a time log. You will soon learn where time is wasted!

Start out with the day and date. Jot down your activities in 15-minute segments. Keep this diary faithfully for a week, and then add up the time segments. How much of your time were you able to spend as planned? Where were hours wasted? What might you have delegated to others?

This is a self-awareness experience that may give you some surprises, but you are not likely to change your habits without desire and direction. If you cannot manage your time well, it is unlikely that you can manage a business well.

After you have faithfully noted and summed up your time habits each day, clarify and write your objectives, and *plan* your time for achievement of these goals. Evaluate your successes and failures daily until good time management is an acquired skill.

Set aside 15 minutes per week for all solicitors (whether for charity donations, magazines, new products, or promotions). For example, ask them to leave brochures and you will advise them of your decision if they return on Thursday at 11:00 AM. If the charity is local, you may have budgeted a contribution and can simply ask for the pledge card and mail it in. Treat differently the goodwill ambassador of a local charity than you do the slick salesperson from an out-of-the-market area. That salesperson has been well trained to get your signature on a contract for a new copy machine, an encyclopedia, a super vacuum cleaner, or a new "sure-fire business-producing" ad writing scheme. Don't let him steal your time!

If interested, review the brochure, ask for the names of brokers who are using it, and check out results before you sign a contract. Remember that a good salesperson like you is the easiest person to sell to—and don't buy what you don't need because you were "sold" by a super salesperson.

The associate who wants a great deal of your time for sharing every experience can be dealt with in different ways. Say, "Instead of telling me, would you write it up?" Or, "I'm working on something important, but I have five minutes if you'll summarize." Then give them your full attention for the time allotted.

One manager I know says, "I have no time for long stories; give it to me in a paragraph."

Develop a technique that is comfortable for you in dealing with this time stealer. Sometimes it is your top producer who feels entitled to more of your time. Or a new or lower producer may need more of your time. It's the delicate-balance principle in effect here, and your strength comes from your overall objectives for the company and your plan to achieve these. Sometimes you might suggest that an associate's "story time" be put off until a coffee break or lunch and you'll hear it then. Discourage personal "chit-chat" in the office.

Develop skills regarding telephone calls from long-winded friends or customers. Help them get to their point, acknowledge that you heard it, and tell them that you have an appointment and will get back to them if you have a solution to their problem. Put them on your call-back list, but limit their "ear bending" to three minutes at the most. "There's a long distance call on the other line" is a useful close.

Analyzing Time Use

A manager's well-planned use of time sets an example for others in the office. Discussing how productively they manage time could be the subject of an office meeting or an individual counselling session. Help them realize how they spend time now by jotting down the approximate number of minutes they spent yesterday on the following:

Contacting clients _____   Other (name) _____
Community activities _____   _____
Calling prospects _____   _____
Showing property _____   _____
Inspecting new listings _____ _____
Researching facts on a   _____
  listing _____   _____
Calling attorneys or   _____
  banks _____   _____
Attending meetings _____   _____
Writing letters _____   _____
Updating listing book _____   _____
Lunch with a customer _____   Planning work for
Office forms _____   tomorrow _____

Do this on a day following a normal workday, and limit the time to 15 minutes. Summarize how the time was spent, review the work plan they have made for today, and help them write out a time management plan for tomorrow. (See Table 11-1.)

Delegating

A major time-saver is delegating jobs that others can do. The manager who cannot delegate probably uses time ineffectively, may have ego needs that require "doing it myself", or may be a perfectionist who is easily dissatisfied with the efforts of others.

List all the jobs to be done. What can be delegated? Assess the capabilities of the persons available. Assign the task, outlining expectations and setting parameters and a target date. For example, if delegating ad writing, specify the objective, areas of media and size choice, deadlines, space, and cost considerations.

Be specific when you delegate. To not set a date for completion of a task is a little like asking someone to come for dinner "sometime".

Thank those who accept such jobs for their efforts. Taking on responsibilities in new areas represents a challenge and an opportunity for growth.

TABLE 11-1   EVALUATE YOUR TIME MANAGEMENT SKILLS

	Yes	No	Could Improve
1. Do you have a written plan each day?			
2. Will you tackle disagreeable tasks first?			
3. Can you limit time wasted on office chit-chat?			
4. Can you help someone "get to the point"?			
5. Do you cluster similar tasks?			
6. Can you tactfully terminate telephone calls when you've conveyed your message?			
7. Can you avoid being a "soft touch" to everyone who asks for donations?			
8. Do you know what your most creative hours are?			
9. Do you set aside some time each day for creative planning?			
10. Are you willing to delegate jobs that can be handled by others?			

If 7 out of 10 answers are "YES", you have a good sense of organizing time.

Have you ever heard any of these excuses for not delegating?

- "If I want it done right, I'd better do it myself."
- "It takes longer to train someone else to do the job than it does to do it myself."
- "Nobody can write ads as well as I can."
- "I'll lose control if I begin delegating."
- "If I delegate this, they'll think I'm lazy!"
- I got where I am today by doing this myself."
- "I'll have to O.K. the final product anyway—I might as well do the job myself."
- "I would delegate, but no one is willing to accept the responsibility."

All of these rationalizations add up to *fear*.

- *Fear* of competition from a subordinate who does the job well.
- *Fear* of blame if a subordinate does the job poorly.
- *Fear* of "I will no longer be needed."
- *Fear* of ego loss when a subordinate finds a better way to do the job.

When You Delegate

Before assigning a responsibility to someone, have an agreement about the job and how and when it is to be done. Choose a person who is willing to do it, and then follow up to see that it is done. An old saying goes: "I have six honest serving men; they serve me well and true. Their names are What and Why, Where and When, How and Who."

As an aid in deciding which jobs might be delegated to associates or to a secretary, write out a list of the jobs you are now doing. Some responsibilities must remain with the owner. Others can be shared by staff members. (See Table 11-2.) When I wrote out my list, I found that many jobs could be delegated and that associates were responsive to the challenges offered.

Decision Making

A good delegator is likely to be the person who can make decisions easily and does not expect to be right 100 percent of the time. If you have a perfect score on decisions, you are probably too conservative, and frightened of taking risks. If you are right only 50 percent of the time, you are probably too daring, and your mistakes can be costly. If you're averaging 75 to 80 percent right, you probably have a good balance between a cool head and a willingness to be innovative. James Robinson, Chairman of the Board of Directors, American Express Company, said, "Do something. Lead, follow, or get out of the way."

Crises You Cope With

The best-planned day can go astray when a crisis arises, and it will. It becomes an immediate problem to be solved. Expect the unexpected; plan for what may go wrong. The Titanic only carried enough life boats for one-third of the passengers . . . "because it could never sink".

While we hope for harmony in all transactions, with a satisfied seller and a contented buyer, problems and complaints will arise. The angry owner storms into your office, blaming the associate and the company and demanding that one or the other pay for what's wrong. An associate may feel angry because the accusations are unfair, feel threatened because of the money demands, or simply become upset. The problem goes to the manager for solution.

Typical problems can include a well that goes dry, a septic system that needs replacement, a furnace that expires, and a tenant who refuses to let the property be shown to buyers despite a show clause in his or her lease.

It's important that the manager stay cool and in control. Review communications skills. If the "injured party" is crying, look straight in their

TABLE 11-2 CHECKLIST FOR DELEGATING

Job	Owner	Manager	Associates	Secretary	Bookkeeper
Establishing policies and procedures	X	X	X		
Company goal setting	X				X
Associate goal setting		X	X		
Budget planning	X				X
Cost controls					X
Recruiting, interviewing	X	X			
Selection of associates	X	X			
Training	X	X	X		
Supervision of associates	X	X			
Termination decisions	X	X			
Activity records	X			X	
Balancing checkbook					X
Writing ads		X	X		
Taking photos		X	X		
Maintaining files				X	X
Transaction records			X		X
Obtaining listings		X	X		
Working with prospects		X	X		
Maintaining supplies				X	X
New material	X	X			
Signs, keyboxes			X	X	
Legal decisions	X				
Conventions, seminars	X	X	X		
Creative planning	X				

eyes; it will be difficult to maintain tears. Let the complainant run out of steam; don't interrupt or get defensive. Marshall your thinking while they unload or, in psychology jargon, "ventilate".

Consider what they are really saying, how they feel, how you feel about it, and what some possible solutions to the problem are.

Take the following precautions to reduce your case load of complaints. Recommend that each purchaser have a termite and a building inspection; include these contingencies in the contract. Recommend several qualified inspectors, and let the buyer choose and make the appointment. But remember, a building inspector does not assume any liability for concealed defects or latent conditions. Wells and septic systems are usually not covered. Sellers can be devious and not inform a listing broker of defects, although a broker is diligent about trying to obtain all the facts and convey them to prospects. It is difficult or impossible to seek recourse from sellers who have left the state. The distressed purchaser looks to the listing or selling broker to pay repair or replacement costs. There is no way a company can afford to fix all the things that can go wrong!

Certainly, if a representative of your company has made an honest error and is responsible, you will assume the expenses of correcting the defect. Chalk it up to experience; the associate will have learned an expensive lesson through sharing the expense. Try to maintain a good relationship with the property owner.

Some real-life cases are cited in Chapter 3. It is essential that all associates understand that decision-making authority with regard to a potential lawsuit is not delegated. Such decisions must be made by the owner after he or she has been informed of all the facts and has consulted an attorney.

Creative Planning

Owners and managers frequently complain that because the day-to-day problems that arise in the office take so much time to resolve, very little time is available for creative planning. Yet we are aware that we should include planning on a daily basis.

In your job as manager —

- One-third of your time should be spent on planning and creativity.
- One-third of your time should be spent executing these plans.
- One-third of your time should be spent in company control jobs.

The more you acquire skills in time management and delegating, the more time you free up for creative planning that will help your company prosper.

Summary

A successful manager can confront a variety of problems daily, sort them out for priorities, and make decisions about possible solutions. He or she knows where to get the facts and has the courage to move ahead, even when he or she encounters obstacles.

A written time organization system is a time-saver. Awareness of time stealers and skill in handling them can be developed.

The willingness to delegate some responsibilities to others can give a manager the time needed for creative planning.

Time management is an acquired skill and takes self-discipline to achieve. The manager's ability to analyze time use, establish priorities, and set up a system for time control can be a big asset as he or she helps associates learn to manage their time effectively.

Review Questions

1. List three things necessary to manage time well.
2. Suggest a time management system that would work for you.
3. Name three time stealers.
4. Why does clustering similar tasks or telephone calls save time?
5. Discuss some obstacles to an ability to delegate.
6. Role-play a crisis situation.

12

Advertising and Public Relations

A big item in the company budget will be advertising and promotion, including the following:

- Classified ads
- Institutional ads
- Property brochures
- Direct mail
- Display ads
- Signs and billboards
- Radio, television, audiovisual equipment
- Give-aways
- Gifts to customers
- Entertaining
- Public relations

Classified Ads

The largest share of the advertising budget usually goes for newspaper classified ads. Management will decide where, when, why, what, and how much to advertise, and will measure the results of the advertising program.

The objective of a classified ad writer is to make the office phone ring. The objective of the agent who answers is to get an appointment to show the property. The agent also gets the caller's name and phone number—a caller who will not give a name is more "suspect" than prospect!

115

Surveys show that the ad headline is what grabs attention and generates calls. In the body of the copy, don't tell too much (the reader may eliminate the property), and use more nouns than adjectives. For example, "30-foot" living room is better than "large" or "spacious" living room.

A big company can afford to dominate classified columns; a small firm must be creative. When one of your bright ideas for a headline produces great results, save it to use again. Examples: "Daffodil Yellow" (spring), "3 Warm Hearths" (winter), "Solar Oriented".

In your marketing area, newspapers may be daily or weekly publications. If a daily, what are key days when ads get answers? Don't spend money without measuring results — keep a log on all ad calls and plan your schedule accordingly. Be sure that the agents who answer your phone are skillful. All agents should know the properties advertised and have "switch sheets". A switch sheet has information on alternate properties that they can describe in brief.

Our Office Advertising Policy

- The ad writer's objective is to make the phone ring, a call from a possible prospect.
- The objective of the person who answers the phone is to get the name and phone number of the caller and to make an *appointment*.
- National statistics say there is 1 chance in 65 that the caller will buy the advertised property. The majority buy something else, even though it costs more. Once we have the prospects out, we educate them on market values in our area.
- Last year it cost us about $200 for a phone to ring on an ad (dividing the dollars spent on ads by the number of calls). Don't blow $200 — *know* the property advertised. Have a switch sheet, ready when you answer the phone. Get the callers name and number and set up an appointment.
- Don't discuss the details of an advertised property with the caller. Mention other properties; get an appointment.
- Don't try to qualify a caller by phone; do it in person.
- SMILE a lot while on the phone.

Institutional Advertising

Institutional advertising promotes the company, not a property. This category includes company ads in professional rosters, community programs, your company brochures, maps, and patron listings for benefits. It's often "good will" advertising; the results are hard to measure. Set a yearly budget for this and stick to it. The Yellow Pages may or may not produce calls; evaluate.

Property Brochures

On a distinctive or unusual property, usually expensive, where you have a long-term exclusive listing, your marketing plan may include a special brochure. Costs will include photographs, typesetting, printing, and distribution. It may range from $200 for a small, black-and-white brochure distributed by an agency, to more than $1,000 for a brochure printed in color for an extensive mailing list.

In our market area, most properties will sell in a 90-day listing period; the unusual may take a year or more. If I plan to invest in an expensive brochure for a unique property, I'd want a year's exclusive contract from the owner. My marketing plan might also include an "open house" where we could show the property to all the brokers in the area. Expensive houses may require expensive marketing plans; protect your investment with a long-term exclusive contract.

Direct Mail

What will you prepare? To whom will you mail it? How often? What will it cost? What is the purpose?

The least costly form of direct mail is in a brochure or "magazine" where supporting advertisers underwrite the cost. You provide the publisher with a mailing list, photos, and copy, and he or she does the rest. Many referral organizations have these "house" magazines. Again, the results are difficult to measure.

If you spend money on direct mail, dare to be different so that what the recipient gets isn't immediately tossed in the wastebasket.

Analyze your direct mail offering: Will it interest the recipients? Will they read it? Does it offer something of value? Is it clear? Concise? Witty? Will they remember the name favorably? How long a time span from in-basket to wastebasket?

Don't waste dollars on direct mail unless your item is worth mailing and will pay off in attention for the cost to create and distribute.

Your mailing list requires updating regularly. You'll also use this list for Christmas cards—or New Year's, Valentine's, Easter, or Thanksgiving cards. Most of us get so many cards for Christmas that I prefer choosing some other holiday for annual greetings from the company and have had amazingly successful responses from our zany New Year's card.

Display Ads

In display advertising, several columns wide, photographs may be used. It costs more than the one-column classified ad, but it can be effective. Try it; measure the results. Magazine advertising is usually of the display type.

Be sure photos to be used are clear and have sharp contrast for black-and-white reproduction. You may wish to use the services of a professional photographer.

One effective way I used display advertising was in the introduction of a new associate of the firm, with her photo and background. It cost little more than mailing out the conventional printed announcement cards. We obtained reprints of the ad from the newspaper and used these in a direct mail promotion to persons outside our area and as an insert in that agent's listing kit.

Signs and Billboards

"For Sale" and "Sold" signs will attract prospective buyers and sellers. Signs should be attractive, well cared for, and properly placed with your name and phone number clearly readable. As with keys and key boxes, the listing agent is responsible for putting up and taking down "For Sale" and "Sold" signs.

The sign outside your office is also important. Keep it in good condition and well lit. Lights may be on a timer switch to go on for key traffic hours only.

Billboard advertising may be effective, depending on your location and market area. Use an expert for design.

Radio, Television, and Audiovisual Equipment

If radio advertising will fit into your budget, do some market research to find which station is most popular in your area. Will you promote the company or specific properties? What are the key hours?

Television advertising may be beyond your budget, but showing properties to prospects on closed circuit television in your office is possible. Audiovisual equipment will cost from $2,000 to $4,000, used or new, in black and white. This includes the camera, videotape recorder, battery pack, and TV monitor set. Extras would include wide-angle and zoom lenses, a long extension cord, lights, etc. It is essential that the users be trained and that the equipment be properly cared for. A town tour by videotape might run 20 to 30 minutes and would be useful in showing the community to prospects. A tape of a house, both exterior and interior, will run only three or four minutes. If agents are not interested in filming their listings, you may need to hire a professional. Advertising that your listings are videotaped for closed circuit viewing may attract sellers, too.

A less expensive audiovisual technique would utilize color slides of the community and of the current listings.

Before you invest in any of these, be sure that there is a program for implementation (who will do what, how, and when).

Give-Aways

Pens, pencils, matchbooks, calendars, and key chains—all with the company name and phone number—are just some of the novelty items available as give-aways. Look for quality, because the bargain pen with your name on it that does not write may reflect negatively on your firm.

Gifts to Customers

Remembering the seller and/or the buyer with a gift after the closing of a transaction may be customary in your area. This is a promotion expense that may be paid by the company, paid by the associates, or shared by both. Your policy manual will cover this; the company budget requires a limit.

Gift possibilities range from taking clients or customers out to lunch or dinner to the following:

- Flowers or plants
- A flowering shrub or tree for a new house (arrange for planting)
- A mailbox for a new house (arrange for installation)
- A subscription to a local paper
- A subscription membership to a local theatre
- A framed photo or ink drawing of house (suitable for reproduction on their Christmas card)
- An engraved door knocker
- Stationary with their new address

Many associates are thoughtful and imaginative in choosing follow-up gifts, although this requires extra time and effort on their part. Following are some examples:

- Taking a picnic basket on moving day, with fried chicken, cold salad, beverages, and paper plates and cups

- Inviting the children out on moving day, taking them to a park or pool
- Dropping by with a bottle of cold champagne and two wine glasses on the first night a couple is settled in
- Giving a "meet your new neighbor" coffee party or brunch
- Inviting newcomers to a buffet supper at the associate's home to get acquainted with people who share their interests, whether bridge, backgammon, tennis, Little League, or PTA
- Maintaining subscription tickets to a local theatre or orchestra group so that the newcomers can be taken as guests

The personal touch is important, whatever the gift. Associates will know whether to show up with a flowering plant or a picnic basket on moving day; whether to invite the newcomer to a tennis or theatre party, a Little League game, a fashion show, or an historical house tour. Our office has a policy that any gift we pay for will be delivered in person by the associate who chose it.

Entertaining

Entertaining at home, whether a small neighborhood coffee party or a large cocktail or dinner party, is good business practice for obtaining future personal referrals. It costs the associate time and money, but it may be tax deductible in part.

Think, too, of gifts that cost nothing but a little thoughtfulness, like a list of babysitters in the neighborhood or an invitation to go to the next Garden Club program or Backgammon League meeting with you.

Let their interests decide the nature of the gift. Some associates are more innovative than others, some more dedicated to the "follow-up". Those who warmly welcome and help to ease the pangs of transition for newcomers definitely establish a repeat and referral source for ongoing business. Future earnings reflect this investment in time, thought, and dollars.

Public Relations

Public relations opportunities are often overlooked as a means to keep your company known in the community. Newsworthy events include being elected or appointed to professional organization offices or committees, attending state and national conventions, attending or teaching professional courses or seminars, and speaking publicly.

Study the newspapers and magazines in your area for the types of articles used. Some may publicize large or unusual properties listed or sold by your firm.

Photographs submitted should be good quality, black-and-white glossy prints — either 4" × 6" or 5" × 7". Professional shots are preferred. If you are speaking at a meeting, for example, you may be able to hire a local newspaper photographer to come and take your picture for a nominal fee.

Associates like peer recognition, too. When they take an educational course, attend a major convention, or serve as a panelist at a meeting, help them use this as P.R.

Press releases should be typed double-spaced on plain paper, with wide margins and space for a heading. Put your name and phone number in the upper left corner. Keep your news timely.

As the firm grows, you may wish to have a Public Relations aide on a retainer basis. Newspaper reporters and/or photographers may be available on a freelance basis. They can advise you on what activities are newsworthy, take the photo, write the story, and submit it to area media. Some dollars expended on good publicity may produce more business than dollars paid for space advertising.

It's good public relations to clip each ad and mail it with a letter to the owners of the property you advertised. Keep them aware of the time and money that you are spending on their behalf.

Opportunities for Public Speaking

If you're asked to speak somewhere, don't modestly decline, feeling that you're not experienced in public speaking. If you're experienced in the subject matter you're covering, and if you prepare your material well, you have something to offer. The advantage for your firm is exposure. The invitation may come from a community group, a Realtor® group, or the local high school having a "Career Day" program. If you'd like to do it, but haven't been asked, volunteer!

The size of the group and the meeting room may determine if you will need audio or visual aids. Will your voice carry to the back row without a microphone? If you are using a blackboard and chalk, will what you write be readable at the rear?

Once your material is prepared, practice saying it. Practice before the mirror, observing what is natural in hand and body movements. Eliminate unnecessary gestures that may be distracting, such as pointing your finger or thumping the table too often. Listen to your voice tones. Are they varied? Do you have a tendency to speak too quickly or too slowly? Can you make eye contact with people in the audience? Always look for a person who's receiving you well. A receptive listener gives you extra energy. Try out your talk on a friend or associate, and welcome their critique.

Should you tell some jokes or not? Some persons do it well; others fail to get a chuckle. Use jokes only to illustrate a point that you wish to make, choosing one that is brief and relative to the subject. Try it out on friends. Did they smile?

Expect to be nervous the first few times. Think of a horse race: any old nag can be led to the starting gate and placidly await the "go" signal. A thoroughbred horse is likely to be nervous and jumpy before the race—but it has a much better chance to be a winner! Be grateful for that extra adrenalin that your system is stirring up when you feel nervous before a speech.

If mechanical or other equipment will be used, arrive early to check this out. You may have requested a podium (with a light that works), a microphone and amplifier, and perhaps a "travelling mike". If you requested an overhead projector and screen, check out the location, visibility, supplies, and ease of operation.

Choose equipment that you'll feel comfortable using. Choices on microphones vary from a stationary one to a hand-held travelling mike to a lavalier attached to your clothing. Ask someone to walk around the room while you test the microphone. Adjust the volume accordingly, but remember that sound does not carry as well in a room filled with people as it does in an empty room.

Finally, to use a joke that relates to making a speech, there was a young man carrying a cello on a midtown Manhattan street. He stopped an older man, carrying a violin case, and asked, "How do I get to Carnegie Hall?" The violinist replied, "Practice, Practice, Practice."

Here are some helpful hints:

- Agree to speak only on a subject that you are familiar and comfortable with.

- Research and prepare your material thoroughly.

- Write out an outline of your talk in a condensed form on 4″ × 6″ cards. Number them in sequence, with key points that you wish to make underlined in color. Don't hesitate to wear your glasses if you need them to follow your outline.

- If you are inexperienced in speaking, request that all questions be held until after you complete your talk. Otherwise, these distractions may get you off your train of thought.

Be sure to send a news release about your talk to the local papers, including a photo of you while speaking if possible. This maximizes the exposure that you have gained, and makes the time that it took to prepare and present the speech well worthwhile.

Summary

Advertising costs usually take the biggest bite out of a budget, and the biggest percentage is spent on classified ads. Skill in writing ads that draw response, a wise choice of which paper to use and what days to use it, and a system to measure results are needed.

If you use direct mail, make it attractive and different enough that it cannot be regarded as junk mail. Company signs should be well designed, sturdy, and well cared for. If you plan to use television or radio advertising, keep a record of the results.

A well-planned public relations program can be less expensive than a lot of advertising, but just as effective. Gifts to a new buyer are part of public relations, and thoughtful attention given to a newcomer by a friendly broker will pay off in future referrals.

Knowledgeable real estate brokers will have (or can generate) opportunities for public speaking. Once you overcome a fear of "getting up in public", speaking skills can be learned. It takes time to achieve proficiency, but the results for me were many invitations to speak at statewide and national meetings.

Review Questions

1. What will be the biggest item in your advertising budget?
2. Why are "For Sale" and "Sold" signs important?
3. Suggest means by which to measure advertising results, and write out a system.
4. Discuss the advantages and disadvantages of spending money on brochures for listings.
5. Write a company policy paragraph on gifts to new buyers, and suggest five possible gifts.
6. What is required for an effective public relations program?
7. Discuss the advantages of acquiring skill in public speaking.

13

Communications and Counselling

The key to a warm and friendly climate in your office will be your skill in communicating and counselling. Rule number one is "Praise in public, criticize in private."

In the January 11, 1977, issue of *Saturday Review* Magazine, Editor Norman Cousins writes: "Human communications is the ultimate art, and we all have a lot to learn."

We need to learn how to communicate verbally with others, both as individuals and in groups. We need skill in written communications — letters, memos, reports. We must school ourselves to be good listeners.

Listening Skill

Develop your listening skill. Listening is a challenge: What am I hearing? How does it fit the facts? What is his or her body language saying? Try to keep your feelings about the person separate from the facts of a session. Be aware of your listening style. Do you interrupt? Jump to conclusions? Tend to dominate discussions? Discover alternate styles.

While we live in a world of outer-space exploration, the area for a manager and associates to explore is inner space — the distance from ear to ear. It's impossible for a really good listener to be unpopular. While listening, ask yourself the following questions:

- What is being said?
- How do I feel about it?
- What is my objective?
- How shall I respond?

This process will make you a better listener.

One-To-One Counselling

Just as an office meeting should have a purpose and a plan, the one-to-one counselling session needs an objective and a plan to achieve it. These sessions may be held on a regular schedule — for example, monthly or quarterly conferences to review the goals set by associate and the X-factor sheet, with the results obtained to date. If an associate is exceeding goals, should they be revised upward? If an associate is falling behind, what's the problem?

Don't try to be the provider of solutions, even if you feel that you know the answer. Ask the right questions; listen carefully to the responses. Help agents define the problem ("a problem well stated is half solved"), and let them come up with their own problem-solving ideas.

Clarify "feeling" and "thinking" questions. "Feeling" questions will be open ended; "thinking" questions are more likely to be close ended.

Open-ended questions improve intercommunication. A basic skill of a good news reporter is to find out —

- Who?
- What?
- Where?
- When?
- How?
- Why?

Note that none of these questions can be answered by a simple "yes" or "no".

Close-ended questions start with verbs:

- Can or can't
- Should or would
- Is or are
- Will or won't

These are likely to get a one-word response.

Both types of questions can obtain facts. Which you use depends on whether you wish to discuss something or merely get a yes or no answer. Associates use words and questions constantly in their contacts with sellers and buyers. Their choice of words can mean the difference between success and failure.

Provide them with opportunities to improve their choice of words and their skill in communicating. Set an example by choosing your words wisely. Study your strengths and weaknesses in communicating. For example —

- Do you use the word "deal" instead of transaction?

- Are hackneyed, meaningless phrases used by associates? "This is the buy of the century." Or "It's a steal at this price!"

Have they heard you use these phrases, or do you set a better example and coach them when indicated?

Sometimes there will be an air of hostility in a one-to-one conference. The associate, client, or customer is wary and untrusting, and seems poised to attack or defend, but not to communicate. The best technique I've learned for this is to copy their body posture. If he is leaning back with one fist on his cheek, I do the same. If he's upright, with both arms on the chair, I sit the same. If he has his fist under his chin, so do I. If he sits back with arms crossed, I copy. This is subtle; the person will not be aware of the technique you are using. But, gradually, the vibrations improve — an attitude of trust takes hold, and real communication can take place.

Solving Slumps

Counselling is called for if an associate is in a production slump. The real estate business is cyclical, with peak seasons, slow seasons, high volume years, and recession effects. You need sellers, buyers, and mortgage money, and may sometimes have a shortage of one or another. When associates are in a "slump", it's easy to blame "lack of listings", "hard-to-satisfy prospects", or "lack of mortgage money".

When half or more of the associates are having satisfactory results from their efforts to list and sell, analyze the problems of the person in a "slump". Is the associate putting the same effort and time into his daily work that he did before? Perhaps a personal or family problem is draining his energy. Maybe he is in a negative, "no luck" frame of mind.

What can the manager do?

1. Become aware of the problem in its early stages; act before it intensifies.

2. Analyze past and present efforts and results.

3. Request conference time and *listen* with care. Remember that only about 25 percent of what is said registers with most people.

4. Ask for his suggestions to solve the problem, and don't interrupt his efforts to grope for answers.

5. Evaluate and discuss his proposed solutions. Associates are likely to suggest more advertising by the firm, joining a franchise or referral system — something that the company can do to turn the associate's "luck" around.

6. Express appreciation for his ideas, but point out that the majority of the associates are doing well under the present structure and advertising plan.

7. Make specific suggestions that may work for him:

a. If it's a personal problem: Suggest that he leave it on his doorstep when he leaves home to go to the office; don't bring the problem to work or discuss it there; free up all his psychic energy and intellect for the job at hand.

b. Go back to basics: Suggest that each day he do the projects he did as a beginner — phone calls, letters, personal contacts. Write a plan; work the plan.

c. Offer some challenges and suggestions: Suggest that he come to the office 30 minutes earlier than usual and stay at the office 30 minutes later than usual. In that extra hour make 10 phone calls a day to past sellers and buyers and to current clients and prospects. 10 calls per day × 5 days = 50 calls. Keep a list of the calls and results to see if there are any leads to sellers or buyers. Set a time limit for a turnaround; try the new approach for two weeks. In two weeks of calling, 100 calls should produce 10 to 20 leads.

d. If he is caught in a trap of defeatism: "Nothing works for me," "Everything's overpriced," "I only get lookers," "I have no luck in getting listings," "You can't trust buyers"—ask *WHY*? You, as manager, have your own insight into the problem; listen for his insight.

If the manager and the associate agree on a plan and work the plan with effort and enthusiasm, good results should follow.

OUTLINE OF A PROBLEM

- Two people + different wishes = A Problem.
- Possible outcomes after discussing:
  a. The problem is resolved.
  b. The problem is not resolved (in fact, it may be intensified).
- Your goal is to resolve the problem; the key is your skill in communicating.
- There are two ways to communicate about the problem:
  a. Honest, open, direct, rational.
  b. Irrational, dishonest, sarcastic, manipulative.*
- If communication is good, it is more likely that the problem will be solved, or that a friendly agreement will be reached that a problem exists.
- Awareness = Options = Moves = Responsibility = Winning on Interactions.

*We cannot get into manipulation because there are at least 300 moves.

An example of a problem that is likely to occur for the manager is when the associate wants to sign up an exclusive listing "at any price", despite a basic management policy of not taking overpriced listings. Communication is needed: between manager and associate; then, associate and seller. Sample dialogue might be:

ASSOCIATE: They're my friends and I can get the listing, but at $175,000. Zilch Company told them to ask that price.

MANAGER: What did you come up with as Fair Market Value from your comparable data form?

ASSOCIATE: It averaged out to $145,000.

MANAGER: So if we accept the listing at $175,000, it's not likely to sell. I assume they'll want us to spend money on advertising?

ASSOCIATE: Of course they want it advertised. They'd like a special brochure!

MANAGER: Our office policy is to not agree to take on the agency for an overpriced listing. We'll be investing our time, money, and effort, and when the property doesn't sell, the owner will feel frustrated, and so will we! Tell the owner this.

ASSOCIATE: But they're friends!

MANAGER: All the more reason to be very open and direct. The owner has options. He should be alerted to these and the likely consequences.

A problem existed and was clarified. It was not resolved at this stage, but open communication took place.

Saying "No" to an associate isn't easy. But there's many a time you have to say it. Be direct and open about your reason for a "No." If the ad budget can't take any more expenses to push his listing, say so. If he wants to hold a fancy catered open house at his new listing and you regard this as a waste of money, say so. Hear the associate out, ask for time to think about it, and when you respond with "No, we can't do this at this time because . . . ", remember the old adage "Be graceful under pressure."

Prospecting

This may be the time to try new business-getting techniques, if the associate is willing. If he or she has never tried "cold" calling or "farming", suggest a plan for this. "Cold" calling is a misnomer when it turns up "hot" leads! "Farming" in the real estate business is so called because it is planting seeds, some of which will germinate and produce business.

If the market survey interview approach appeals to the associate, work out a sample interview and role-play it several times so that the associate will feel comfortable about doing it. Rather than calling it canvassing or "cold" calling, call it "prospect research". The objective is to obtain leads to property owners who wish to sell, leads to persons who would like to buy, and news of neighborhood changes. Calling may be easier if the associate can leave a small gift. To encourage calling, the firm may want to share in this expense. There's an old saying, "Leave your gift and leave", so calls can be brief.

Excellent books and tapes are available to help agents develop good "farming" techniques. Select some that are appropriate for your marketing area, and encourage associates to use them.

Communication Cycle

When a conference is needed, request the agent's time with courtesy, fitting your time to the associate's busy schedule. Be specific; ask for five minutes or a half hour, depending on the purpose and plan. Give your full attention to the person, eye-to-eye contact, no interruptions. State your purpose. The sender of a message has *intent*; the receiver has *attent*.

You cannot control the behavior patterns of another person. To each his own, the power to change. But how you communicate can affect the other person, and change is always possible. Send a clear message, with good strong vibes of intent and interest. Listen carefully to responses. Feed back what you hear. If your message is not understood, repeat, rephrase. Keep your cool about the purpose of the meeting, even if the response feels negative or defensive. As you quietly listen, recall the demands made on agents: the long and uncertain hours, the frustrations of lost transactions, the lack of security, the team effort required.

The purpose of the session may be to determine why an associate's production has fallen behind the goals set. State the purpose; invite the associate's attention. You may have some key questions to ask: Are there family or health problems? Were your goals unrealistic? Are outside interests too time consuming?

If it is a situation where termination is a very real possibility, state this, and set a time limit for change in work habits and results.

Strive for agreement that your message has been received and understood and that the lines are open for communication. Don't expect any miracle from counselling—expect to state or to inquire, to hear, to test for feedback that your message was received clearly. At the end of the conference, each should know where the other stands.

SENDER ⟶	RECEIVER
"My message is . . ."	"I hear you saying . . ."
becomes	*becomes*
RECEIVER ⟵	SENDER
"I hear you saying . . ."	"My message is . . ."

Empathy—the ability to understand and share in someone's feelings—stands you in good stead here. Use your empathy but retain your objectivity on purpose and plan. If you go mushy with sympathy, the problem will not be solved.

Thank the person for hearing you, for the time and attention. The receiver's obligation is to listen and communicate back. Communication skills can be improved with practice; you can learn to be assertive in a productive way.

The parties may not agree, but they can acknowledge having heard one another's point of view.

Barriers

Barriers to good communication include:

Overuse of pat phrases or cliches

- "As a matter of fact . . . ."
- "You know, ..."
- "It goes without saying . . . ."

Self-disparaging remarks

- "My opinion isn't worth much, but . . . ."
- "Maybe I don't know what I'm talking about, but . . . ."
- "If you don't mind my telling you . . . ."

Dishonest remarks

- "I don't mean to tell you what to do, but . . . ."
- "I shouldn't tell you this, but . . . ."
- "I hate to say this, but . . . ."
- "I'll make this short, but . . . ."
- "It's not for me to say, but . . . ."
- "Not to change the subject, but . . . ."
- "Just one last word . . . ."

Manipulative remarks

- "If it's not out of your way . . . ."
- "If it isn't too much trouble . . . ."
- "If it isn't asking too much . . . ."
- "If it weren't for me . . . ."

Sarcastic remarks (which are anger in disguise)

- "I suppose your alarm didn't go off."
- "Sorry you find it hard to get here on time."
- "I'm thrilled you have such a busy social life that there's no time for the office!"

Resistance to Change

As you communicate in office situations, you will encounter the barrier of resistance to change. Typical objections to a new idea or system being introduced may be:

- "It'll never work."
- "Why do we have to change the way we've been doing it?"
- "Somebody else tried that."
- "No one else is doing it."
- "Why doesn't the Board appoint a committee?"

Expect to encounter this resistance to change. Recognize barriers to communication as you hear them. Don't press for your proposed change when several associates are negative toward you idea. Listen to their comments carefully. Be diplomatic, not dictatorial. Keep lines of communication open.

Verbal Communication

Simple, direct, honest communication is a skill worth learning. Listen to yourself and observe the areas that need improvement. Learn to send clear messages to the receiver, without disclaimers. Watch out of for "if's", "but's", and "that's." Use "I" statements wherein you state your opinion and take responsibility for it. For example:

- "I like your new haircut" is a clear statement to the receiver, likely to be warmly received.
- "You got your hair cut" is a statement, but not an "I" statement, and it leaves the recipient wondering.

Simple "I" statements include:

- "I feel badly when your customers are kept waiting because you're late."
- "I feel angry when someone calls on an ad and the agent doesn't know the property."

- "I get upset when long distance telephone calls go on too long with needless chit-chat."

Body Language

Communication does not depend on the spoken word. Body language also sends a message. Study body language, which is nonverbal communication. For example, in either a one-to-one or a group conversation, the following may be observed:

- A lifted eyebrow that says: "Why?"
- A jutted chin that says: "Show me!"
- A wince that says: "Message not favorably received."
- A smile: "I agree."
- A nod: "I hear you."
- A pull on the ear: "I'm thinking."
- A frown: "I don't like it."
- A shrug of the shoulders: "That's the way it is," or "Of no interest to me."
- A clenched fist: "I'm fighting."
- Arms folded: "I resist you."
- Hand tapping on table: "Get on with it."
- Open hands: "I'm willing to hear you."
- Closed hands: "I have reservations."
- Leaning forward: "Tell me more."
- Leaning back: "I'm not convinced."

In a group situation, a wink communicates the intimacy of a shared response to what's been said.

Learning to observe and interpret body language can be fascinating and help you in communicating skills.

Sometimes you'll get a double and conflicting message—one verbal, one nonverbal. Which are you to believe? An example is the tapping fingers of the person who says he's not in a hurry. The nonverbal signal is likely to be more accurate than the polite verbal message.

A major reason for poor communication is a lack of clarity and shared understanding of terminology. An example of the confusion in terminology that exists within the real estate industry is the way the words *co-broke* and *referral* are used interchangeably. No co-brokerage is possible except under the terms of a listing agreement. The listing broker may "co-broke" a

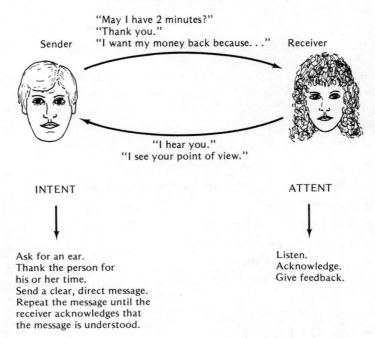

COMMUNICATION CYCLE

"May I have 2 minutes?"
"Thank you."
Sender   "I want my money back because. . ."   Receiver

"I hear you."
"I see your point of view."

INTENT   ATTENT

Ask for an ear.   Listen.
Thank the person for   Acknowledge.
his or her time.   Give feedback.
Send a clear, direct message.
Repeat the message until the
receiver acknowledges that
the message is understood.

property with a subagent. A prospect to purchase may be "referred" to another broker, but no contract exists between the prospect and the referring agent. Letters of agreement about acceptance of a referred prospect should be exchanged between the "sending" and the "receiving" firms, so that no misunderstanding arises as to the terms of acceptance in the event that a prospect buys.

Written Communication

Written communications require clear intent as much as verbal communications do. Ask yourself, is this letter, memo, brochure, or report necessary? Why? What do I intend to accomplish and how? If I expect a reply, have I made this clear to the receiver?

Letters should be brief and to the point. When you write letters, memos, or reports, ask yourself—

- Is there a good reason for it?
- Is my message clear?
- Will my objective be achieved by this, or does it need follow-up?
- How will I implement this communication to reach the objective?

Printed communications, like your company or community brochure, may require professional help to create and write. Determine the quantity needed, the means of distribution, and the image you wish projected, and consult an expert. Get comparative estimates on printing costs, and don't be caught with 2,000 out-of-date company or community information brochures in your storage closet.

Letter Writing

Letter writing is referred to, sometimes, as a "lost art". It's easier for many to pick up a telephone to contact someone. But there are advantages to a letter, when it's neatly typed or written on good-looking company letterhead. It's likely to be read by both husband and wife, and it may be read more than once. It's a visual reminder of your name and can be more effective than verbal communication.

When you spend some time composing a letter, and are pleased with your efforts, save a copy for the "Sample Letters" file. With a change of names and dates, it can be used as a model the next time that you have a similar reason to write someone else. A skillful secretary can be in charge of seeing that the indicated letters get out.

EVALUATE YOUR COMMUNICATION SKILLS

	Yes	No	Could Improve
1. Can I maintain control of the interview by asking appropriate questions?			
2. Can I handle uncomfortable confrontations objectively?			
3. Do I avoid sarcasm and anger?			
4. Am I effective in conveying my message?			
5. Are my criticisms always constructive?			
6. Am I alert to nonverbal messages?			
7. Can I remain objective, not emotional, in human communication?			
8. Can I control my feelings of tension if I am under pressure?			
9. Can I create an atmosphere of trust and mutual respect?			
10. Am I a good listener?			
11. Do I evaluate what I hear before responding?			
12. Do I check for feedback?			

If 12 answers are "YES", you're a supercommunicator!

Handwritten notes on attractive notepaper may be sent by associates, preferably those whose handwriting is clearly legible. Be sure that the company name, address, and phone number are subtly on the notepaper.

Summary

Skill in communicating is a highly valuable asset. Becoming a good listener is paramount. Develop the ability to listen attentively, evaluate what you hear, and read the messages being sent by body language.

Counselling sessions need an objective and a plan to achieve it. Close-ended questions tend to keep such a session brief. Open-ended questions will be more provocative.

The communicating cycle involves sending a message and checking for feedback to determine if the message was heard as it was intended. Awareness of barriers prevents you from falling into the trap of making disparaging, dishonest, or manipulative remarks.

Written communications can waste time and money unless you have a specific purpose and have mastered the techniques to achieve it. Well-written letters create a favorable image for your firm.

Review Questions

1. Why is being a good listener important? Discuss three aids to developing this skill.

2. Explain the difference between *open-ended* and *close-ended* questions.

3. Role-play a counselling session with an associate whose productivity is well below average. Evaluate your strengths and weaknesses.

4. What is *feedback*?

5. Name five barriers to good communications.

6. Suggest ten body language signals.

7. Why and when is a well-written letter more effective than a telephone call?

8. Write a sample letter to clients asking for a renewal of their listing that is about to expire.

Growth Decisions

Most small businesses follow a bell curve of growth and development to the height of their success, then they decline — in percentage of the market, in staff, and in profits.

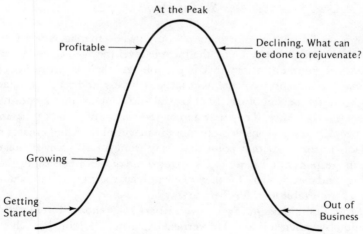

Another way to describe the stages of the rise and fall of an enterprise is:

INVEST

TEST

CREST

NEST

DIVEST

- You'll *invest* your time and money.
- You'll *test* your marketing area and company performance.
- You'll reach a profitable *crest* and try to *nest* there, continually striving to maintain a productive position.
- If, despite your best efforts, the enterprise fails, you'll *divest* your interests.

The planning that is an important part of a manager's job must include both short- and long-range objectives.

Perhaps in year one, you plan to capture 10 percent of the market in your area, and by year two, you plan to have 15 percent and be showing a profit. Where do you plan to be five years from now?

The company must change with changing times. What are successful competitors doing that you're not doing? Are you continually taking courses, attending seminars, looking for ways to grow? How "big" do you want to be?

An organization chart of a typical small office may look like that on page 139.

Status Quo

We all have different comfort zones. Many owner–managers feel satisfied with a small office. They enjoy the income level they've achieved and the closeness of communications that is possible. As their business increases, they may add one or two more associates each year and reach the stage of an eight- to ten-person office. If successful and content, they'll continue to manage this size office. They may add on too many and find that having 12 to 15 people requires considerably more managerial time and creates more problems to solve. At that point they may want an assistant manager to share the responsibilities and to take over some of the supervision, record-keeping, and cost control. Or they may cut back the staff size to what they feel is a comfortable level for them to stay on top of.

More ambitious and aggressive owners may choose to enlarge their operation by either horizontal or vertical expansion. Adding branch offices in other marketing areas is horizontal expansion. Diversification into specialized fields of real estate, all under the same roof, is vertical expansion.

One of your agents may want very much to be a manager—he wants your job, or the opportunity to manage a branch office for you. An old war general's saying is, "In every private's pack lies a Marshall's baton." If he knows the new marketing area and is willing to be trained in managerial skills, opening a branch office with him as manager may be an excellent investment. Define his role and responsibilities, agree on how he is to be compensated, and plan a training program for him.

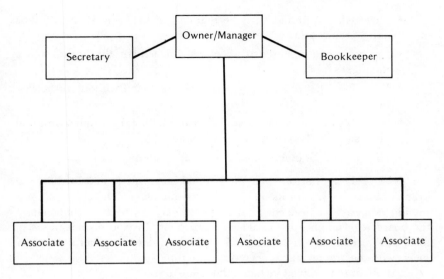

Organization Chart for Small Office

Horizontal Expansion

The most common growth decision is to open branch offices in other marketing areas. The owner will carefully analyze the marketing potential in another area and the locations and staff available; he or she will recognize the need for a qualified and trained manager in each office. The owner needs venture capital for start-up costs and maintenance expenses until the new office becomes established and makes a profit.

As in opening the first office, the owner has options: to acquire or merge with an established firm or to start from scratch. Scrutinize keenly what the competition will be.

Among the questions to ask before making this growth decision are the following:

- Is the area located near enough that the company name and image will be recognized and useful?
- Has the marketing potential been researched?
- Is a well-trained, competent branch manager available?
- Is the branch manager knowledgeable about the area?
- Can the branch manager attract and train good associates?
- Does the branch manager have guidelines for achieving the results expected by the owner?

- How will communications be maintained between the head office and a branch office?
- Have spheres of authority been established for the branch office manager's job?
- Is it clear what he or she can and cannot spend without authorization?
- If the branch manager is also listing and selling, how much time will he or she spend on management functions?
- How will the branch manager be compensated?

New challenges arise when you expand horizontally and own several branch offices, each with its own residential manager. The chain of command changes. In a large corporation the owner may become chairman of the board with another stockholder as president. Instead of meeting with associates directly, as in a small office, the president or general manager meets with the branch managers most of the time.

Problems to be solved included the following:

- A need for systems that ensure control
- Difficulties in communications
- A need for central files
- Tight cost controls
- A training program for managers
- Clear delineation of spheres of authority and what decisions will be made only by the owner

There may be more income, in time, but there's likely to be a loss of autonomy and a feeling of being "out of touch" with all the people who are associated with the company.

The organization chart of a typical multi-office company may look like that on page 141.

_____ *Vertical Expansion* _____

Growth of the company by the addition of departments specializing in diversified fields of real estate, other than residential, will require additional space in the building and someone who is an expert in the particular discipline being added. Areas of diversification may include Appraising, Commercial/Investment, Counselling, Construction of New Homes, Land Development, Insurance, Rentals and Property Management, Conversion of Apartment Buildings into Condominium Units, Remodeling and Sale of Older Homes or Time-Shared Units (in vacation areas).

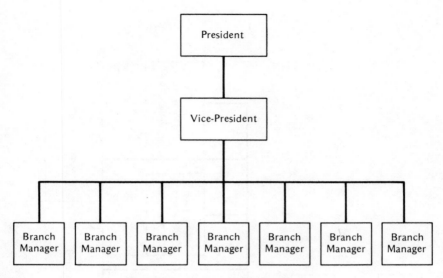

Organizational Chart: Horizontal Expansion

The potential of each division should be carefully analyzed for advantages and disadvantages before adding the extra space and qualified personnel required.

Questions to ask before diversifying include the following:

- What lead-in time will be required before the new division shows a profit? (In Commercial/Industrial, for example, it may take two years.)

- More secretarial and bookkeeping help will be required. What will it cost?

- Does the agent in charge of the division have the specialized training, knowledge, and skills necessary?

- Does the department head expect a fixed salary?

- If considering a subdivision development and new house sales, what will it cost to furnish a model home and keep it staffed for showings?

- Will there be problems over a conflict of interests when one of the residential agents has a friend interested in commercial or investment property? How will you handle this?

- What will it cost to add more space, buy the furnishings and equipment, advertise the new division, and pay salaries?

- What systems and controls will be established?

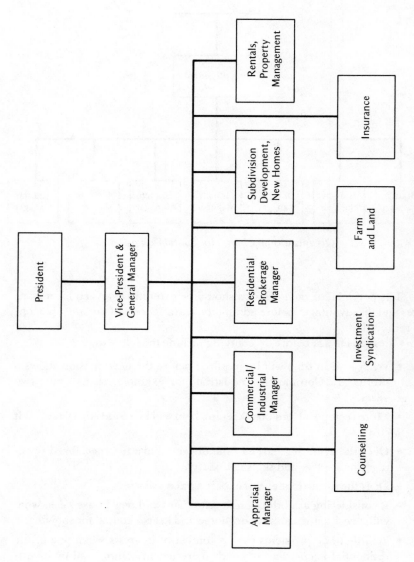

Organizational Chart: Vertical Expansion

As you consider all your options and the amount of capital you are willing to risk, you may conclude that you prefer to remain a residential brokerage office and to stay where you are if you can accommodate enough staff in your established location.

The organization chart of a typical diversified office may look like that on page 142.

Shared Desks

Some firms find themselves in a situation where the location is excellent, the firm is growing, more associates are needed, and interior space cannot accommodate more desks. To move or not to move?

Moving is costly; no desirable location may be available; and the company image will suffer if sellers and buyers get inadequate service because you're understaffed. One option is to assign more than one associate to a desk, all using central files. They have one drawer to call their own and can stagger hours of "desk use". An office meeting to pose the problem and work out some solutions is called for.

100% Commission

A recent innovation in some areas is the 100% commission system. The office owner provides the necessary office space, overhead expenses, and management expertise for a set monthly fee to each associate. Associates pay the advertising costs on their listings and their own promotion and telephone expenses. The associate receives the entire commission check at closing. There is generally a fee to join the company, an "up front" sum to the owner from each associate.

This plan sounds attractive to experienced producers who can afford the initial fee to join and are confident of steady income for the monthly assessment. The advantages to the owner are the ease in budgeting because income is known; expenses include the manager's salary and the owner's profit.

A system of controls and records must be maintained, and policies and procedures planned and implemented. What are the associates' expectations from management? How much supervision will be required? As all will be working under your company name, your reputation is at stake. Estimate how much clerical help will be needed.

Associates may be eager to join initially, and the owner has the "up front" profits. If there is a turn-down in the market, they may not be able or willing to remain, and the owner may encounter overhead cost deficits.

The concept has worked well in some areas, failed in others. It fits a medium-size company (15 to 20 agents) better than a small company, because a normal turnover rate does not upset the budget.

Franchises

When you are approached to join a real estate franchise, you have a choice of staying an independent entrepreneur and doing business strictly under your own name and methods, or of joining a group.

Some advantages of joining may be access to —

- Identification with a big name.
- Regional or national advertising on radio, television, etc., that a small firm could not afford.
- Recruiting and training services provided by the franchisor.
- An established referral system.
- Reduced expenses through volume purchasing.

Some disadvantages may be —

- The high cost to join, plus a percentage of your gross income annually, and advertising assessments in addition.
- The failure to achieve marketing and advertising objectives due to poor management or insufficient capital of the franchisor.
- The required affiliation with brokers in the chain whose standards of service do not meet your needs and preferences.
- The loss of your own identity in your market area as you promote the franchise organization.

To sum up — there are pros and cons, and when approached, research them thoroughly.

Referral Organizations

Regional and national referral organizations abound, soliciting firms to join their network. The premise is based on profit from mobile America, where 20 percent of the population moves every year and a certain percentage will move beyond your marketing area.

Can you refer the transferee to another area and earn a referral fee? National organizations provide rosters and promotion kits; they may have a company magazine for each area represented, a format for registering transferred prospects from A in one state to Z in another, and a central office.

There is usually a fee to join — an agreed-upon percentage of the referral fee — and dues or fees to maintain membership. Some organizations hold conventions and training seminars, and advertise nationally. Check out the results from other brokers in the referral organization. How many qualified prospects were received? Was a quota required on Referrals Out? What are ongoing monthly costs? Will more than one company be used in your market area?

Referral organizations serve a useful function, but consider carefully before you invest in membership. Some are broker owned and operated, based on a broker-to-broker referral fee principle; some are "third party" organizations.

Third Party Companies

This is basically a company that provides referral services and equity funding to assist corporate transferees. The equity funding program enables the seller to transfer title to a home-buying corporation, thereby getting funds to permit him or her to purchase property in the new job area before the previous home has been sold.

Some organizations employ "corporate callers" who solicit business from large corporations and underwrite the transfer of property for a fee from that company. The benefits to a corporation are these: not having corporate capital tied up in houses and easing the change of location process for the transferee, getting him or her on the new job faster and with fewer headaches.

Brokers with negative opinions of third party companies seem to say, "Here's someone who has his hand in two brokers' pockets, the sending broker and the receiving broker, and all he has is smarts in merchandising — no experience in the real estate business."

Don't knock it — they provide a useful service to companies, transferees, and brokers. An affiliation may be profitable to you.

Rejuvenation

In my experience, many fine companies were started and were brought to a peak of success (measured in terms of number one in listings, number one in sales) because the entrepreneur had so much to give in time, energy, effort, ability, creativity, risk taking, sensitivity, and alertness to change.

Company decline set in as that owner began to give more time to other affairs — perhaps state and national association work or community organizations — or just took more time off for travel or hobbies. No plan was made for the ongoing success of the firm in the owner's absence.

Be aware that there will come a time to turn the reins of management over to someone younger and more energetic than yourself. Don't wait too long to step aside gracefully, to take in a partner, to hire a manager, or to sell the company. You may negotiate an arrangement with a new owner whereby you are paid as a consultant for a number of years. But go on to your golden years with someone else in charge of running the successful company that you built up.

Partners and Retirement

As your business grows, you may wish to take on one or more partners in the company. If you have been an individual entrepreneur or sole proprietor, you may wish to incorporate, establish a value for the shares of stock, and sell off shares to enterprising and valued associates who want "a piece of the action". The manager of a branch office, opening under your name, auspices, and experience, may wish to own part of the parent company. Establish criteria for possible partners, including their years of experience and proven capability and loyalty. Ask your accountant to determine the value of the company so that shares can be priced.

If you wish to maintain control, you may want to retain 50 percent of ownership. Consider this when you plan on partial or full retirement. You may offer a plan whereby a large part of their stock purchase will come from their pro-rated shares of the company profits over a period of several years.

Clarify expectations on their part and yours, define responsibilities and how decision making will be shared, and write out your mutual agreements. Consult an attorney on a buy-back arrangement should the associate leave.

Summary

Most management decisions are made day to day for "here and now". Growth decisions differ because they involve long-range planning and the investing of both capital and time in researching the facts needed to make a wise decision.

The odds are stacked against venture capital invested in opening a real estate office. But many owners welcome the challenges of expansion and enjoy the added responsibilities. They are willing to acquire the knowledge and skills needed.

Each growth decision presents certain problems to be solved and a choice of solutions. Among the options are expanding horizontally or vertically, joining a franchise or a referral system, or staying "small" if it's comfortable and profitable for you.

Excellent courses and books are available that explore various growth options in depth, and a prudent investor will take advantage of this knowledge. The heedless will cry all the way to the bank when faced with closing out a poorly researched expansion or obtaining another loan to keep going.

Review Questions

1. List five growth options available to the owner of a small firm.

2. Discuss factors to be considered before investing capital in opening a branch office.

3. Name three problems that will arise when the firm has branched out into other marketing areas.

4. List five areas of diversification into related real estate fields other than residential brokerage.

5. How do you arrive at an estimate of the amount of venture capital required if you decide to expand horizontally?

6. Suggest three added expenses that the firm will have when adding a new division to your present office.

7. List three advantages and three disadvantages of joining a franchise system.

8. What factors would influence the decision that it is time to retire, hire a manager, take on a partner, or sell the firm?

Appendix

Code of Ethics;
*NATIONAL ASSOCIATION OF REALTORS®**

REVISED AND APPROVED BY THE DELEGATE BODY OF THE ASSOCIATION AT ITS 67TH ANNUAL CONVENTION NOVEMBER 14, 1974

Preamble . . .

Under all is the land. Upon its wise utilization and widely allocated ownership depend the survival and growth of free institutions and of our civilization. The REALTOR® should recognize that the interests of the nation and its citizens require the highest and best use of the land and the widest distribution of land ownership. They require the creation of adequate housing, the building of functioning cities, the development of productive industries and farms, and the preservation of a healthful environment.

Such interests impose obligations beyond those of ordinary commerce. They impose grave social responsibility and a patriotic duty to which the REALTOR® should dedicate himself, and for which he should be diligent in preparing himself. The REALTOR®, therefore, is zealous to maintain and improve the standards of his calling and shares with his fellow-REALTORS® a common responsibility for its integrity and honor. The term REALTOR® has come to connote competency, fairness, and high integrity resulting from adherence to a lofty ideal of moral conduct in business relations. No inducement of profit and no instruction from clients ever can justify departure from this ideal.

In the interpretation of his obligation, a REALTOR® can take no safer guide than that which has been handed down through the centuries, embodied in the Golden Rule. "Whatsoever ye would that men should do to you, do ye even so to them."

Accepting this standard as his own, every REALTOR® pledges himself to observe its spirit in all of his activities and to conduct his business in accordance with the tenets set forth below.

Article 1

The REALTOR® should keep himself informed on matters affecting real estate in his community, the state, and nation so that he may be able to contribute responsibly to public thinking on such matters.

Article 2

In justice to those who place their interests in his care, the REALTOR® should endeavor always to be informed regarding laws, proposed legislation, governmental regulations, public policies, and current market conditions in order to be in a position to advise his clients properly.

Article 3

It is the duty of the REALTOR® to protect the public against fraud, misrepresentation, and unethical practices in real estate transactions. He should endeavor to eliminate in his community any practices which could be damaging to the public or bring discredit to the real estate profession. The REALTOR® should assist the governmental agency charged with regulating the practices of brokers and salesmen in his state.

Article 4

The REALTOR® should seek no unfair advantage over other REALTORS® and should conduct his business so as to avoid controversies with other REALTORS®.

Article 5

In the best interests of society, of his associates, and his own business, the REALTOR® should willingly share with other REALTORS® the lessons of his experience and study for the benefit of the public, and should be loyal to the Board of REALTORS® of his community and active in its work.

Article 6

To prevent dissension and misunderstanding and to assure better service to the owner, the REALTOR® should urge the exclusive listing of property unless contrary to the best interest of the owner.

Article 7

In accepting employment as an agent, the REALTOR® pledges himself to protect and promote the interests of the client. This obligation of absolute fidelity to the client's interests is primary, but it does not relieve the REALTOR® of the obligation to treat fairly all parties to the transaction.

Article 8

The REALTOR® shall not accept compensation from more than one party, even if permitted by law, without the full knowledge of all parties to the transaction.

Article 9

The REALTOR® shall avoid exaggeration, misrepresentation, or conceal-ment of pertinent facts. He has an affirmative obligation to discover adverse factors that a reasonably competent and diligent investigation would disclose.

Article 10

The REALTOR® shall not deny equal professional services to any person for reasons of race, creed, sex, or country of national origin. The REALTOR® shall not be a party to any plan or agreement to discriminate against a person or persons on the basis of race, creed, sex, or country of national origin.

Article 11

A REALTOR® is expected to provide a level of competent service in keep-ing with the Standards of Practice in those fields in which the REALTOR® customarily engages.

The REALTOR® shall not undertake to provide specialized profes-sional services concerning a type of property or service that is outside his field of competence unless he engages the assistance of one who is competent on such types of property or service or unless the facts are fully disclosed to the client. Any person engaged to provide such assistance shall be so identified to the client and his contribution to the assignment should be set forth.

The REALTOR® shall refer to the Standards of Practice of the National Association as to the degree of competence that a client has a right to expect the REALTOR® to possess, taking into consideration the complexity of the problem, the availability of expert assistance, and the opportunities for experience available to the REALTOR®.

Article 12

The REALTOR® shall not undertake to provide professional services concerning a property or its value where he has a present or contemplated interest unless such interest is specifically disclosed to all affected parties.

Article 13

The REALTOR® shall not acquire an interest in or buy for himself, any member of his immediate family, his firm or any member thereof, or any entity in which he has a substantial ownership interest, property listed with him, without making the true position known to the listing owner. In selling property owned by himself, or in which he has any interest, the REALTOR® shall reveal the facts of his ownership or interest to the purchaser.

Article 14

In the event of a controversy between REALTORS® associated with different firms, arising out of their relationship as REALTORS®, the REALTORS® shall submit the dispute to arbitration in accordance with the regulations of their board or boards rather than litigate the matter.

Article 15

If a REALTOR® is charged with unethical practice or is asked to present evidence in any disciplinary proceeding or investigation, he shall place all pertinent facts before the proper tribunal of the member board or affiliated institute, society, or council of which he is a member.

Article 16

When acting as agent, the REALTOR® shall not accept any commission, rebate, or profit on expenditures made for his principal-owner, without the principal's knowledge and consent.

Article 17

The REALTOR® shall not engage in activities that constitute the unauthorized practice of law and shall recommend that legal counsel be obtained when the interest of any party to the transaction requires it.

Article 18

The REALTOR® shall keep in a special account in an appropriate financial institution, separated from his own funds, monies coming into his possession in trust for other persons such as escrows, trust funds, clients' monies, and other like items.

Article 19

The REALTOR® shall be careful at all times to present a true picture in his advertising and representations to the public. He shall neither advertise without disclosing his name nor permit any person associated with him to use individual names or telephone numbers, unless such person's connection with the REALTOR® is obvious in the advertisement.

Article 20

The REALTOR®, for the protection of all parties, shall see that financial obligations and commitments regarding real estate transactions are in writing, expressing the exact agreement of the parties. A copy of each agreement shall be furnished to each party upon his signing such agreement.

Article 21

The REALTOR® shall not engage in any practice or take any action inconsistent with the agency of another REALTOR®.

Article 22

In the sale of property which is exclusively listed with a REALTOR®, the REALTOR® shall utilize the services of other brokers upon mutually agreed upon terms when it is in the best interests of the client.

Negotiations concerning property which is listed exclusively shall be carried on with the listing broker, not with the owner, except with the consent of the listing broker.

Article 23

The REALTOR® shall not publicly disparage the business practice of a competitor nor volunteer an opinion of a competitor's transaction. If his opinion is sought and if the REALTOR® deems it appropriate to respond, such opinion shall be rendered with strict professional integrity and courtesy.

Article 24

The REALTOR® shall not directly or indirectly solicit the services or affiliation of an employee or independent contractor in the organization of another REALTOR® without prior notice to said REALTOR® .

Where the word REALTOR® is used in this Code and Preamble, it shall be deemed to include REALTOR®-ASSOCIATE. Pronouns shall be considered to include REALTORS® and REALTOR®-ASSOCIATES of both genders.

The Code of Ethics was adopted in 1913. Amended at the Annual Convention in 1924, 1928, 1950, 1951, 1952, 1955, 1956, 1961, 1962, and 1974.

License Requirements by States

1981 NARELLO Interstate Report	Education and Experience Requirements				
	Salesperson's		Experience Required for Broker's License	Broker's	
	Prelicensing Education	Continuing Education		Prelicensing Education	Continuing Education
Alabama	45 cl hrs	None	2 yrs full time	45 cl hrs or 15 sem hrs if app. has less than 2 yrs experience	None
Alaska	None	None	2 yrs	None	None
Arizona	45 hrs	12 hrs per year	3 yrs	90 hrs	12 hrs per year
Arkansas	30-hr course must be comp. in 1st yr	None	2 yrs	90 or 30 hrs	None
California	None	45 hrs every 4 yrs	2 yrs	18 sem hrs	45 hrs every 4 yrs
Colorado	48 cl hrs	None	2 yrs active lic	96 cl hrs	None
Connecticut	30 cl hrs	None	2 yrs active lic	90 cl hrs	None
Delaware	75 cl hrs	None	5 yrs	30 cl hrs	None
District of Columbia	None	None	None	None	None
Florida	51 cl hrs	14 hrs every 2 yrs	1 yr	48 cl hrs	14 hrs every 2 yrs

Source: 1980 NARELLO Annual Report, National Association of Real Estate License Law Officials, Sunset Valley Law Building, 2580 South 90 Street, Omaha, Nebraska 68124, issued January 1, 1981.

Notes: Hours mean classroom hours in an approved course. Many states also require photos, fingerprints, credit reports, and posting of bond. Contact the real estate license commission in a specific state for an application form and current requirements.

Education and Experience Requirements

1981 NARELLO Interstate Report	Salesperson's		Experience Required for Broker's License	Broker's	
	Prelicensing Education	Continuing Education		Prelicensing Education	Continuing Education
Georgia	24 cl hrs or 5 qtr hrs	80 hrs 1st 2 yrs, then 6 every 2 yrs	3 yrs active lic	60 cl hrs or 15 qtr hrs	6 hrs every 2 yrs
Hawaii	30 hrs	None	2 yrs	40 hrs	None
Idaho	45 hrs	None	2 yrs act lic or may accept ed or allied ind exp	90 hrs	None
Illinois	30 hrs	None	1 yr as sales.	90 hrs	None
Indiana	40 hrs	None	None	64 hrs	None
Iowa	30 hrs	7 hrs annual	1 yr	None	7 hrs annual
Kansas	None	60 hrs	2 yrs	None	90 hrs
Kentucky	96 hrs	None	2 yrs—1 yr if assoc. deg. in R.E. or bac. deg. w/maj in R.E.	336 hrs	None
Louisiana	50 hrs	15 hrs every 2 yrs	2 hrs as sales.	120 hrs	15 hrs every 2 yrs
Maine	None	12 hrs	1 yr	90 hrs	12 hrs
Maryland	45 cl hrs or 3 sem hrs	12 hrs	3 yrs	135 cl hrs or 9 sem hrs	12 hrs
Massachusetts	24 hrs	None	1 yr	30 hrs	None
Michigan	None unless fail 1st time; then 30 hrs	None	3 yrs	90 hrs	None
Minnesota	30 hrs pre-licen. 60 hrs w/in 1st yr of licensure	45 hrs every 3 yrs	2 yrs	90 hrs	45 hrs every 3 yrs

Education and Experience Requirements

1981 NARELLO Interstate Report	Salesperson's		Experience Required for Broker's License	Broker's	
	Prelicensing Education	Continuing Education		Prelicensing Education	Continuing Education
Mississippi	6 sem hrs	None	1 yr	12 sem hrs	None
Missouri	40 hrs	None	Must be sales.	40 hrs	None
Montana	None	None	2 yrs sales.	None	None
Nebraska	60 hrs	None	2 yrs sales. & 120 hrs ed	120 hrs w/2 yrs exp.; 180 hrs w/no exp.	None
Nevada	90 hrs	20 hrs 1st 2 yrs; 10 hrs every 2 yrs	2 yrs act	24 coll lev crdts.	20 hrs 1st 2 yrs; 10 hrs every 2 yrs
New Hampshire	None	None	1 full yr or 2000 hrs part-time	None	None
New Jersey	45 hrs	None	2 yrs imm. before app.	90 hrs	None
New Mexico	60 hrs	None	None	180 hrs	None
New York	45 hrs	45 hrs	Yes	90 hrs	Yes
North Carolina	30 hrs of equiv. exp.	None	2 yrs as sales. or 60 hrs ed	60 hrs or equiv. exp	None
North Dakota	30 cl hrs w/in 1st yr of licensure	None	2 yrs	90 hrs	None
Ohio (1980)	60 hrs		30 consum. trans. & 2 yrs as sales.	60 hrs	None
Oklahoma	45 hrs 7/1/81 30 hrs	21 hrs every 3 yrs eff 7/1/84	1 yr	45 hrs 7/1/81 30 hrs	21 hrs every 3 yrs eff 7/1/84

Education and Experience Requirements

1981 NARELLO Interstate Report	Salesperson's		Experience Required for Broker's License	Broker's	
	Prelicensing Education	Continuing Education		Prelicensing Education	Continuing Education
Oregon	90 hrs	24 – 2 yr lic	3 yrs	150 hrs	24 – 2 yr lic
Pennsylvania	60	None	3 yrs	240 hrs	None
Rhode Island (1980)	None	None	1 yr as sales.	90 hrs	None
South Carolina	30 hrs or 1 yr lic in another state	None	None	60 hrs or 2 yrs exp	None
South Dakota	30 hrs	24 – per 2 yrs	2 yrs	90 hrs	24 – per 2 yrs
Tennessee	3 hrs	3 hrs	2 yrs	6 or 90 GRI	3 hrs
Texas	315 hrs	None	2 yrs	540 hrs	None
Utah	90 hrs	None	3 yrs full-time lic or equiv	150 hrs	None
Vermont	None	None	1 yr as sales.	None	None
Virginia	45 hrs	None	3 yrs	135 hrs	None
Virgin Islands	None	None	2 yrs	45 hrs or 2 yrs exp	None
Washington	30 hrs prior to 2nd renewal	None	2 yrs in last 5 yrs	90 hrs prior to taking exam	None
West Virginia	90 hrs	None	2 yrs	180 hrs	None
Wisconsin	30 hrs w/in 2 yrs of licensure	10 per 2 yrs	None	60 hrs	10 per 2 yrs
Wyoming	None	None	2 yrs as act sales. or deg in R.E.	None	None

Affidavit

A F F I D A V I T

I, _____ , depose and say that
I am associated with _____
as an independent contractor.

In this status I will pay all my own license fees; all dues to
the Board of Realtors® and any other organizations to which I choose
to belong; all automobile transportation and insurance expenses; all
entertainment expenses.

It is understood that I pay my own income and social security
taxes; nothing is withheld from my commission checks.

I am not required by the firm to maintain any listing or sales
quota, attend office meetings, or maintain any specific schedule.
I can schedule my holiday and vacation time without consulting the
firm.

I receive no minimum salary, sick pay, or any other company benefits,
except that _____ (minor sales aids,
optional).

It is agreed that the company will provide desk space, training,
and suggest methods to achieve results from my efforts. I am free to
choose my own methods, so long as I am ethical.

Termination may be by either party upon notice of at least thirty
days. Each party shall be entitled to all fees and commissions which
accrued prior to termination.

_____
(Signature)

Sworn to before me this _____ day
of _____ 19 _____ .

_____
Notary Public

Associate Compensation and Tax Certificate Form

Associate Compensation and Tax Certificate Form

1. Name _____

2. Address _____

3. Social Security Number _____

4. Calendar Year _____

5. Total Commission Income Received _____

No federal income tax or Social Security taxes were withheld from these commissions. The taxes due were reported by me on my tax return described below and have been paid in full.

6. Name and address shown on tax return:

   _____

7. If a joint return was filed, spouses's Social Security number

   _____

8. Service center where filed _____

9. Commission shown in Item 4 above was reported on Form 1040

   (a) Line _____ Page _____

   (b) Schedule _____

   If reported on Schedule C, F, or SE, Self-Employment Tax of

   $ _____ was paid.

I declare the above information is true, correct, and complete to the best of my knowledge and belief.

10. Signature _____ Date _____

Power of Attorney

POWER OF ATTORNEY

     KNOW ALL MEN BY THESE PRESENTS, that I, _____(name)_____,
of the Town of _____, County of _____, and
State of _____, do hereby appoint _____(name)_____,
of _____, as my attorney-in-fact to
act in my name, place and stead in any way I myself would do, if I were
personally present, with respect to _____
_____,
including but not limited to _____.
     Hereby ratifying and confirming all that my said attorney may do
or cause to be done.
     IN WITNESS WHEREOF, I have hereunto signed my name and affixed
my seal this _____(day)_____, _____(month)_____, _____(year)_____.
In the Presence of:

_____   _____(signature)_____

_____

STATE OF _____)
                             : ss. _____(town)_____
COUNTY OF _____)

   The foregoing POWER OF ATTORNEY was acknowledged
before me this _____ day of __(month)__, __(year)__, by __(signer)__

_____
Notary Public
My commission expires:

Promissory Note

PROMISSORY NOTE

$2,000.00

_____
(date)

FOR VALUE RECEIVED, I promise to pay to the order of Anne Andrews,
of Main Street, Hometown, PT, the sum of $2,000.00 (Two
thousand and no/100 dollars) with interest from the date of
_____, on unpaid principal at the rate of
_____ per cent per annum.

Principal and interest are due and payable on the first of every
month with installments of $_____ per month beginning
_____(date)_____ and continuing until such principal and
interest have been paid.

This note may be prepaid in whole or in part at any time without
penalty.

In event of default on any installment payment, the entire note is
due and payable at once. If legal action is necessary to collect
this note, the borrower agrees to pay all costs of collection in
addition to sums due.

(Signed)

_____
(borrower)

_____
(address)

Witnessed:

_____

Rotation Record

Name	Prospect	Source	Date	Results
Ann	James Scott	N.Y.T. ad on Hughes	10/3	Likes Curtis!
Bob	Robert Sienna	called	10/5	Wants Land
Chris	Bernard Kizer	Walk-In	10/6	One floor only - Good
Donna	Mrs Betty Springer	Condo ad	10/7	needs 4 R
Ann	Rockwells	c/o Joe V.	10/7	May buy down
Bob	Baxters	Sign on Ross Land	10/10	too expensive
Chris	Liz Keeler	Friend of DB's	10/11	Will wait till June
Donna	M/M Clyde Goodwin	Referral HBAC	10/13	Int. in O'Brien
Ann	Dr. Coggiano	c/o - Payne	10/14	Must be near hosp.
Bob	Paul Walters	Benson Ad in F.P.	10/17	likes - too far at
Chris	Owen & Nancy Williams	Drews recommended us	10/17	must sell house first
Donna	Schwartz	phone call	10/19	needs mother-in-law room
Ann	D. McKenzie	Referral JCR	10/20	Good - wife here - in 2 weeks
Bob	Tarkington	Herald ad on Solar	10/21	Wants to build
Chris	Charles & Martha Cook	Former B.H. customer	10/21	likes Marshall
Donna		VACATION		
Ann	Virginia Sweeney	Ans ad on Bergen	10/23	Wants a Pond
Bob	J. Chappell	Walk-In	10/23	N.G.
Chris	Strong	Phone Call	10/24	Got Listing!
Donna	Mr & Mrs H. Mendoza	C/B Stretcher	10/25	Must be near stores
Ann	M/M Wallace Caldwell	"Mini-Estate" adv	10/26	Has horses
Bob		Hospital		
Chris	Linda & Roger Tomlin	P.R. story in Bulletin	10/27	Rented Holmes
Donna	Rossi	Ad on Nichols	10/27	Prefers newer house

Policy and Procedure Manual

Introduction

Introduction

A successful real state brokerage firm must have high professional standards and a favorable reputation in the community. The purpose of this policy manual is to aid associates in creating and maintaining this favorable reputation. Each associate *is* the firm when dealing with the public and can use the manual as a guide. The policies are intended to promote close cooperation among all members of the firm. The joint thinking of the firm members is represented, and the policies are open to review and discussion. Associates are invited to offer suggestions to improve the operations of this office. Our policies have been developed and proved successful by the experience of many Realtors® over the years.

Successful real estate operations depend upon personal factors that are associated with good leadership and freedom of enterprise. Under this concept, the associates of our company are treated as entrepreneurs in their chosen field of real estate. They can expect good planning and friendly assistance from management. Individual alertness, enterprise, and resourcefulness will determine the rewards an associate can earn under this system.

The affidavit and tax certificate form help associates maintain their status as independent contractors.

I.   Broker–Associate Relationship

    A. The following are required of associates:
1. License and bond
2. Membership in the Board of Realtors®
3. A car that is kept presentable and adequately insured
4. To give priority to their business interests
5. To work diligently for the benefit of the firm
6. To adhere to the Code of Ethics of the National Association of Realtors®, and to the bylaws, rules, and regulations of the local Board of Realtors® and its Multiple Listing Service.

    B. The firm will furnish the following:
1. Office and desk space
2. Office telephone
3. Multiple Listing Service membership of the Board of Realtors®
4. A consistent program of advertising
5. Training in listing and sales skills
6. Consultation when unusual problems arise.

    C. Associates are expected to share cheerfully in the office work which has to be done and in keeping the office looking neat and attractive. An alert, pleasant staff is our most effective means of building good public relations. Personnel are expected to receive all clients with the utmost courtesy and a sincere desire to be of service, whether the client is theirs or someone else's. Associates are expected to share with each other any knowledge of listings and to assist others whose lack of experience might prevent them from successfully obtaining a listing.

    D. Today's professional associate is an expert who is willing to give his or her time and knowledge to bring buyers and sellers together for their mutual benefit. Professionals succeed because of their knowledge and skill, and not by the use of high pressure tactics. Our company believes both buyers and sellers are entitled to careful, considerate counselling. The same high standards of conduct and ethics we apply to our clients must be used with each other.

II.   Basic Office Policies
Clear policies are needed in order that clients and customers may be properly cared for.

A.   Our office is open from 9:00 a.m. to 5:00 p.m., Monday through Saturday.

B.   Associates can arrange to pro-rate and share office coverage so that one associate is available as needed.

C.   Each of us should try not to disturb or interrupt anyone unless it's urgent.

D.   It is preferable that lengthy discussions of personal problems do not take place in the office.

E.   Associates may not obligate the firm for any expense without permission of the management. Should legal expenses arise from a case involving a transaction, the cost is shared by the associate and the firm. The firm reserves the right to decide when to institute legal action. Our policy is to avoid litigation whenever possible.

III.   Offers, Deposits, Receipts, and Transactions

A.   Our standard receipt form is used for offers and acceptances. Any change must be initialed by both parties.

B.   A copy of the contract should be obtained from the attorney. All details of a transaction should be recorded on the form provided as soon as possible.

C.   The firm maintains a trustee account that will be used to hold escrow funds.

D.   All offers should have an earnest money deposit. All offers are submitted to sellers. In the event that two associates have offers on the same property, both are submitted—we do not decide for the owner.

E.   No property is "off the market" until there has been a "meeting of the minds"—an offer and acceptance.

IV.   Commissions

A.   *Charges to Clients.* Rates of commission have been established by management. Acceptance of a promissory note in lieu of a cash commission must be agreed to by the owner of the office.

B. *Listing and Sales Commissions Paid to Associates*. The associate shall receive 50% of the net commission retained by the office within one week of the office's receiving the commission check.

C. *Disputes*. Associates are expected to work out their own agreement on how the commission is to be split when a prospect is shared or turned over from one associate to another. In the event a controversy between associates is brought to the attention of the management, the decision of the manager shall be binding upon both parties.

D. *Referrals*. When a referral is sent to us by a cooperating broker, clarify the referral agreement at that time.

V. Other Services

Because our firm places great emphasis on service to our clients, we offer the following diversified services in addition to the listing and sales of vacant land, houses, condominium units, and commercial properties:

- *Rentals*: fee established by management.
- *Property management*: fee set by management.
- *Appraisals*: fee set by management; fee may vary depending upon the amount of time and work involved.
- *Financing* (by maintaining good sources of mortgage loan money from banks, savings and loan associations, and insurance companies): no charges are made by our firm for this service.
- *Construction advice*: a no-charge service.
- *Investment counselling*: to be done by qualified personnel only and normally for a fee set by management.
- *Special sales promotions* (such as brochures, etc., on certain exclusive listings) are expensive. None may be promised to a seller without the approval of management.
- *Land planning, subdivision assistance*: consult with management who will establish a fee based on the amount of work involved.
- *Referrals* throughout the country as well as within our county and state.
- *Equity funding* (or "bridge loans"): under certain circumstances.

VI. Prospect Policy and Commission Schedule

Our overall aim is to see that all prospects are promptly and cheerfully served, and that associates help each other to bring about sales.

Our policy is that a direct prospect who asks for A—or who came to the firm because of A—should always be handled by A, if possible. When someone asks for or refers a new prospect to A, every effort should be made to set up an appointment for A. But if A is away, or cannot be reached, the prospect goes on office rotation, and the commission is shared according to agreement.

Who cares for an associate's prospects when he or she is on vacation? Ideally, if Broker A is leaving on vacation, she will go through her prospect cards and discuss the status and needs of her people with one or more associates (what prospect should be called if *x* type house is available, etc.). Those who need attention should definitely be "turned over"—but leave the cards on the original associate's desk so that information can be located quickly if a prospect suddenly calls or comes in. There are "shared" prospects as well as "turned over" prospects, depending on varying circumstances such as a pending sale, customer wishes, etc. Basically our policy is that "the customer is always right." The prospect may wish to return to A after working with B in A's absence, or may wish to continue working with B. Our commission schedule tries to apportion commissions fairly, so that each associate is compensated for time and effort, but in the event of a conflict of opinions, the decision of the manager will be final.

When A takes out a prospect and sells, the commission split of 50% to the associate and 50% to the office is very simple. But every time an associate's share must be split with another associate who assisted in the sale, a precedent is established. Associates who have participated in sharing servicing of a prospect that has led to obtaining a listing or a sale inquire eagerly of the manager what they will receive at closing. A ready reference schedule saves a lot of time.

ASSOCIATE SHARE OF COMMISSIONS

	A	B
1. A has been working with a prospect; A is not available, so B shows and sells	50%	50%
2. A's prospect is serviced more than once by B when A is unavailable, but A sells	90	10
3. Prospect asks for A (never met); A is not available, so B shows and sells	10	90
4. Friend of A wants to list his house; A is on vacation, so B obtains listing; A services on return	90	10
5. Prospect calls or comes in on ad; he doesn't ask for A, although he has been out with A; B services and sells although A is available.	10	90

It's important that we review this page of the manual once or twice a year because associates may wish to change the way their share of the commission is split. When the majority agrees on a change, this will be noted on the page, including the date of the revision.

VII. Listing Policy

   A. We believe that our multiple listing service is an excellent marketing medium for owners and present MLS to all owners positively. When an MLS offering of our office is sold by another office, the listing associate receives 50% of the MLS fee paid to the firm.

   B. Land tracts on which the broker obtains a new, nonexclusive listing: The listing associate has one week to contact area builders who are the most likely prospects. After that, the lister gets 10% of the saleperson's share of commission if it is sold by another associate in the firm.

   C. Houses on MLS: If Broker A turns in an MLS offering, and it is sold by any broker in this office, the same MLS fee is deducted and paid out to the listing associate as if the house were sold by some other firm.

   D. Our MLS listings are exclusives, but we occasionally obtain "open" or nonexclusive listings for the office. When one of these is sold, the same percentage of the commission is paid to the listing broker as if it were an MLS.

   E. Our fee for listings varies; the fee may be shared with other brokers on a basis of 20%, 30%, or more. Every listing shall clearly state what our listing fee is.

   F. All listing contracts come under the recent "Plain Language" law enacted by the Connecticut legislature in 1980.

VIII. Selling Policies, Aids, and Procedures

   A. Listings: All listings must be in writing and signed. We have forms for MLS, nonexclusive, and land listings. An MLS kit is available with samples of every form used.

   B. Records: Each associate keeps on hand the following:
      1. Prospect file
      2. Blank forms (MLS, open listings, deposit, transaction)
      3. Listing book (include rentals and land)
      4. Map of our marketing area
      5. Financing information

C. Log: Record in the office log information on —
1. New listings.
2. Sold listings.
3. Inquiries and wants.
4. Financing information.
5. Appointments.
6. Anything else needed to keep all associates informed of new developments.

D. Telephone Call Book: The person answering the phone should log all calls in the book. Associates should check the book for calls as soon as they come in.

E. Floor Time: To equalize the amount of office time, each associate assumes certain hours. This is also an opportunity to catch up on paperwork and to do some creative thinking. Things to do include the following: sending letters to prospects, making follow-up reports to listing owners, writing thank you cards, making calls to new owners, studying listings, filling in incomplete listing data, checking financing sources, preparing work plans and reports, and studying. The secretary may answer the phone when in the office; preferably the broker who's next in line for a prospect answers.

F. Answering the Telephone: It is essential that each associate have inspected all advertised properties before answering the phone; it reflects negatively on the office when an associate is unable to describe a property. If it is a call from a referring broker for an appointment to show, try to set it up for the person whose turn it is. If a prospect comes in (or if it is a long, direct phone call), so that a rapport is established between prospect and duty broker, the available associate should carry on and count it as his or her next turn. If the caller is an owner calling to list, make an appointment to list the property.

G. Caddy: The purpose of the "caddy box" on your desk is to distribute new prospects equally on rotation. Prospect inquiries will be cared for by the caddy broker, and when the prospect is taken out, the name goes on the rotation list. There are three exceptions:
1. Prospects for vacant land. (Enter only if a purchase is made.)
2. Rental prospects are not entered until they have agreed to lease a property shown.
3. When we advertise an unusual house priced so far below

average that it could not be duplicated, the prospect will be entered only if he or she agrees to purchase this one-of-a-kind property (or if he or she becomes a prospect for a house in the average price bracket). If the associate who has the "caddy" symbol on his or her desk is not in, the person next up on the rotation list should be available.

H. Nonfloor Productivity: When you are next in line for floor time and/or caddy, be ready and available. Call in before leaving your house if you are en route to the office. If inspecting or calling on someone, give a phone number where you can be reached. Always be ready for unexpected clients. Noncaddy, nonfloor hours can be spent productively inspecting, working on listing files, getting information and land listings from the town hall, seeing builders, etc. But let the office know where you can be reached and/or give a definite return time which can be reported to your prospects who call.

I. Open Houses: It is customary on our board for the listing broker to hold an open house at a newly listed house to allow inspection by all members of the board. It is the responsibility of the listing associate—

  • To notify MLS members of the time, place, and date.
  • To place our open house sign on the property so Realtors® can find it easily.
  • To be on hand to show the house, with a map of the property and any other pertinent information available.
  • To bring our sign back to the office.

The owner need not be at home; it is not customary to serve refreshments.

  As your listings are your stock in trade, try to attend all open houses; always leave your card.

J. Days Off: Days off are chosen on a regular basis. Let the office know if you are available for calls or not. If you wish to switch days, make an interoffice arrangement with someone who will be available.

K. Buying and Selling for Own Account: Any property bought or sold by an associate for his or her own account must be listed with the firm, and full listing commissions, co-brokerage commissions, and other expenses must be paid. No transaction may be made that would reflect negatively on the firm.

L. Office Meetings: These meetings will be scheduled periodically.

Our January meeting outlines goals and plans for the year.

M. Real Estate Board: Attendance at all meetings is strongly recommended. A strong Realtor® board is one of your greatest assets.

N. Follow Up: The office may reassign any prospects or leads for whom suggested action and/or follow ups are not carried out promptly.

O. Follow Through: We do not "drop" the buyer once he or she has closed. The sales associate should call at the buyer's home, and follow up from time to time to see that all is well. Your remembering your buyer will pay dividends.

P. Competitors: Competition is good for us—don't ever knock it; it keeps us on our toes. We always cooperate with our fellow Realtors.® We are much less likely to lose sales through outside competition than from inside sloppiness or laziness. Business always goes where the service is best. If everyone helps to see that our firm gives the best service, we'll always succeed.

Q. Customer Register: All prospects should be listed in this register to help anyone who answers the phone to know whether or not one of our brokers is already working with the caller.

R. Referrals: Occasionally the same prospect will be referred to us by more than one out-of-town broker. Let each one know that we will honor the cooperating broker who actually schedules a specific appointment for the prospect with our office, but that we cannot recognize more than one referring broker.

IX. Education

We believe strongly that the educational opportunities available through your board, your state association, and the national institutes are well worth taking. Education combined with experience increases your competence and professional standing. To stop learning is to stop growing as a human being.

X. Termination

In the event the broker–associate relationship is terminated by either party, the associate will return to the office all listings, forms, records, keys, and any supplies furnished by the office or pertaining to sellers or buyers. On any commissions due under contracts or leases signed while the associate was affiliated with the firm, the associate shall receive his or her share when the check is received by the firm. No profit-sharing plan shall be in effect for associates who are no longer a part of the company. The board of Realtors® and the state license commission shall be notified at once of the change of status.

MAIN STREET • HOMETOWN, PT 00000 • 111-111-1111

CONFIRMATION OF PROSPECT REFERRAL

TO: _____

_____

_____   DATE: _____

Name _____

Address _____

Home Phone _____ Business Phone _____

We will do our very best to satisfy the needs and wishes of this
prospective buyer, and agree to send your office a referral fee of 30%
of the net sales commission due our office as soon as we receive a check.

We honor all referrals for a period of six months from date of first
appointment with the prospective buyer. If, by any chance, this prospect
should arrive at our office through the efforts of another referring
broker, we shall, of course, be obligated to recognize that source as the
referring broker.

We shall keep you advised of our progress with this prospect and trust that
a successful sale will result.

Sincerely yours,

MAIN STREET • HOMETOWN, PT 00000 • 111-111-1111

LAND LISTING

Date _____

I wish to list property located at:

_____

consisting of _____ as shown on _____.

This listing shall be in effect for a period of _____ months.

In the event that the above described property is sold by _____

_____, I/we agree to pay them a commission in the amount

of _____% of the accepted sales price.

This agreement is subject to Sec. 53-35 of the General Statutes as

amended (Public Accommodations Act).

LISTED PRICE: _____

_____ (L.S.)

_____ (L.S.)

_____

Listing Broker for _____

177

Anne Andrews & Associates

MAIN STREET • HOMETOWN, PT 00000 • 111-111-1111

NONEXCLUSIVE LISTING

Date _____

I wish to list property located at _____

Owner's address _____ Phone _____

Tenant name and phone (if any) _____

Type _____ Year Built _____ Builder _____

Exterior _____ Color _____ Land _____

First Floor _____

Second Floor _____

Lower Level _____

Attic _____ Basement _____ Garage _____

Heat _____ Est. Ann. Cost _____ Hot Water _____

Key _____ To Show _____

Walls _____ Insulation _____ Floors _____

Laundry _____ Porch/Deck _____ Storms/Screens _____

Equipment Included _____

Other Buildings _____ Well _____ Septic _____

Mortgage _____ Assessment _____ Taxes _____

Date of Occupancy _____

For Sale or Rent at a Price of _____ Commission _____

This listing shall be in effect until _____

This agreement is subject to Sec. 53-35 of the General Statutes as amended
(Public Accommodations Act).

Remarks:

BROKER: OWNERS:

    S/_____   S/ _____
       for   S/ _____

178

MAIN STREET • HOMETOWN, PT 00000 • 111-111-1111

AGREEMENT WHEN BUYER PAYS COMMISSION

AGREEMENT, made this   day of   19_ _ between
                           of Wilton, Conn., hereinafter called
the REALTOR, and   of
alone, or with others, hereinafter called the BUYER.

WITNESSETH:

WHEREAS, The BUYER has engaged the REALTOR to be his agent in
the negotiations and purchase of real estate owned by:
                          hereinafter called the SELLER.
        SAID real estate is at
and is further identified on Survey Map as:

WHEREAS THE REALTOR, a Connecticut licensed Real Estate Broker,
is and shall continue to perform these services as the BUYER'S agent,

NOW, therefore, the BUYERS Agree to pay the REALTOR
percent of the purchase price of said SELLERS' property when they take
title or, should they assign said contract, at the time of said
assignment, to said real estate.

_____   _____

_____   _____

Market Comparable Form

BASIC PROPERTY DATA	STYLE	SQ. FEET	RMS	BED RMS	DEN	BATHS	GAR	AGE	LOT SIZE	Special Terms &/or Features	DAYS ON MKT	LISTING PRICE	CURRENT SALE OR LIST PRICE
SUBJECT ADDRESS 152 Tower Road	Col.		8	4		2½	2	12½	2Ac.	Fireplace in living room			
COMPETITIVE PROPERTIES FOR SALE NOW													
12 Alexander Drive	Col.		8	4		2½	2	14	2.88	Lovely street, screen porch	30	$165,000.	
62 Spring Street	Col.		9	5		3	2	14	1.8	1 fpl, 5th bedroom redecorated, lovely	60	$169,000.	
201 Club Pines Road	Col.		8	4		3	2	18	2.03	private property	40	$176,500.	
6 Lakeview Road	Col.		9	4	yes	2½	2	15	1.9	Charming, no basement 2 fireplaces	60	$177,500.	
ESTIMATE AVG. VALUE													$172,000.
RECENTLY SOLD PROPERTIES													
358 Westover Road	Col.		8	4		2½	2	12	1.8	Good condition, cul-de-sac	37	$168,000.	$162,500
48 Pearl Street	Col.		9	4	yes	2½	2	13	1.05	Special mortgage Convenient location	45	$169,500.	$162,000
41 Alexander Drive	Col.		8	4		2½	2	5	1.88	Immaculate condition	88	$169,500.	$167,000
65 Painter Road	Col.		8	4		2½	2	13+	2.04	Caught in bad market and winter	90	$162,500.	$150,000
APPROX. INDICATED VALUE													$160,000.
EXPIRED/OFF MARKET PAST 3 MONTHS													
21 Waverly Lane	Col.		8	4		2½	2	6+	2Ac.	Finished playroom in basement	364	$210,000.	
APPROX. INDICATED VALUE (Less Than)													

ADDITIONAL INFORMATION RELATED TO SUBJECT PROPERTY

BUYER APPEAL
1. Location ____
2. Good condition
3. Broad family appeal
4. ____

Market Demand ____ Fair ____

DRAWBACKS
1. Proximity to proposed Route 7
2. ____
3. ____
4. ____

Economic Conditions ____ Fair ____

INDICATED PRICE RANGE

Top Competitive Market Value	$172,000.
Lowest Competitive Market Value	$160,000.
Probable Final Sales Price	
Suggested Starting	

LS Form I Conn. Assoc. of Realtors

180

Training Aids

X-FACTOR OBJECTIVES

X-FACTOR OBJECTIVES FOR THIS YEAR

_____
                                            Associate

_____
                                                Date

This year I plan to earn a total of $ _____.

....

I.   I expect _____% of earnings from listings or $ _____.

     . Average net listing fee is _____ so I must have

        _____ sold listings.

     . Assuming 80% of my listings will sell, I will need

        _____ this year or _____ per month.

     . As I get one listing out of every three presentations,

        to obtain my goal I must make _____ presentations

        or _____ per month.

....

II. I expect _____% of earnings from sales or $_____.

     . Average net sales commission is _____ so I must

        have _____ sales or _____ per month.

     . Assuming one in five prospects will buy, I will

        need _____ prospects or _____ per month.

....

III. I expect that about 50% of these prospects will be personally

     referred to me. I will need to obtain the others through

     _____.

Reviewed: _____   Signed: _____
                                               Associate

MONDAY	TUESDAY	WED.
Turn in Benson MLS + put Key Box on	write ad F.P. on Hudson	write Benson ad for Sunday NYT
Call Carlsons / who ind action	Pick up leases for Parker 4R	10 AM haircut
CALL:	See Dep to Trustee	Baby present for Schroeder's ?
RIDGEFIELD-60min NYC MLS Realtor ... Contemporary Spacious 4-bedrm, 2 bath home located on wooded 3½ acres, Liv rm w/flr-to-ceil bkcs, eat-in kitchn, family rm w/ flrce, Cathearl ceil in 14x24 master bedrm. Avail for immediate occupancy. $113,000.	11 AM Open Houses Wallace	
P.S.B.a Dalton 34 Peach Tree 842-3907 Call back 8/22	Huston Ricardo Benson	12:30 Lunch with Polly Gordon at OLIVER'S ($16)
2 P.M. Smith Closing F.C. Bank	Write the Jones in Cleveland, send train schedule	
	2 PM Meet Bank Appraiser @ Pierce House	Call Hendersons
pick up dry cleaning!!	order more cards	
		P. + Z. Mtg.
	Take a plant to Smith's	Robinson Subdivision 8pm

THURS.	FRIDAY	SAT.
		9:30 McKenzie Bldg site
9AM BOARD MTG.	Hudson ad -- clip + send	for SOLAR house
Call Tom Brown @ IBM 229-4000 ext. 2710	Call Hills	lunch at Red Barn?
10:30 Hills trace map on Armstrong	Pick up photos 11 AM - OPEN HOUSES Carrington Nelson	2PM Tom + Jill Brown
		SUNDAY
3PM Historical House Tour — take Mrs. Smith	Make apptmts: Browns Parker Waterhouse Nelson ??	ad on Benson in NYT — sure to send
	Dinner with Carolyn	

Role-Plays for Training Sessions

1. *Objective*:   To achieve skills in qualifying prospects

   Roles: Trainee = Associate
                     Trainer = Difficult prospect

   Scene: Prospect enters office, newspaper in hand . . .

PROSPECT: "I want to see the house with red shutters."

TRAINEE: (Must respond appropriately, introduce self, obtain Prospect's name, begin to qualify)

PROSPECT: "Just show me the house with the red shutters. I haven't much time."

        (Trainer must ask tough questions, may be rude, tries to dominate the interview, appears unwilling to disclose financial information—hams it up in the role of a difficult prospect.)

Sample questions:

"Does this house have a basement?"

"What's the percentage of high school graduates who go on to college?"

"Is there a waiting list for the country club?"

"How far is a shopping center from this house?"

"What's the crime rate in the area?"

"What will my taxes be like on a house like this?"

"How big are the bedrooms?"

"Do all the fireplaces work?"

"Is there public transportation?"

        (Evaluate the trainee on how smoothly the objections are used to advantage and how far he or she gets in qualifying the difficult prospect.)

2. *Objective*:   To achieve skills in overcoming objections when showing a property

   Roles: Trainee = Associate showing house
                     Trainer = Prospective buyer

   Scene: Associate escorts Prospect to property . . . Prospect raises objections.

PROSPECT: "There's only a one-car garage."

"The master bedroom looks small."

"It looks to me like they've had water in the basement."

"See the crack in the dining room ceiling?"

"Are they going to leave the refrigerator?"

"It's pretty high priced."

(Evaluate the trainee on responses to objections, creativity in problem solving, attitude, patience, and results. Has the house been presented fairly and the seller's interests well-represented?)

3. *Objective*:   To achieve skills in negotiations

   Roles: Trainee = Associate
   Trainer = Alternately, buyer *and* seller

   Scene: Associate is submitting an offer to the seller and succeeds in obtaining a counteroffer to submit to the buyer.

ASSOCIATE: Mr. Seller, my prospect for your house wants to submit an offer. He's a qualified buyer, but he has some reservations about the heating costs and lack of insulation, and he's taken these costs into consideration.

SELLER: Yeah, what's the offer?"

ASSOCIATE: You requested an end-of-June closing; he prefers the end of August. But he's willing to compromise on this. He will require a building inspection and a mortgage contingency. Financing should not be a problem; he's a qualified buyer.

SELLER: Well, how much? What's his offer?

ASSOCIATE: His offer is $125,000—contingent on a building inspection and obtaining a mortgage.

SELLER: That's a pretty low offer; our house is on at $135,000.

ASSOCIATE: I realize that, but he does like the house and is a qualified buyer. I suggest you give him a counteroffer.

SELLER: Hum---, I don't know. We're moving and wouldn't want to wait until the end of August to close. How about we split the difference? He agrees to close July 1st and I'll sell him the place at $130,000.

ASSOCIATE: I'll submit this counteroffer to the potential buyer immediately.

(Next the associate talks to the prospective buyer.)

ASSOCIATE: Good news! The Sellers made a counteroffer. However, they do not wish to close later than July 1st.

BUYER: They wouldn't accept $125,000?

ASSOCIATE: No—they feel their house is worth more. They've agreed to sell it to you for $130,000. This is Fair Market Value, in my opinion. Your family does like the house and the location, and I feel it's an excellent investment.

BUYER: But the closing on our house isn't until August!

ASSOCIATE: I'm confident we can arrange a swing loan so you can take possession of your new home sooner.

BUYER: Well, why don't you offer him $126,000? Or $126,500?

ASSOCIATE: He has already met you halfway, the market is active at present, and I feel $130,000 is a very fair price.

BUYER: Okay, see if we can wrap it up.

What Can We Do For You?

As an owner attempting to market your home yourself, you can —

1. Decide what you'd like to get for it.
2. Put an ad in the paper.
3. Put out a "For Sale" sign.
4. Stay by the phone.

. . . Or You Can List Your Home With Us

1. We have a professionally trained full-time sales force.
2. We provide a phone that's answered 24 hours a day.
3. We have an office open seven days a week.
4. We underwrite planned advertising programs.
5. We can expertly qualify prospects to screen out the "tourists" and the financially unsound.
6. We will schedule appointments for every showing.
7. We make arrangements for showing when you are away.
8. We will provide professional advice on pricing your home.
9. We have knowledge of current market values, trends, and conditions, and many years of marketing experience.

10. We prepare a market-comparable data analysis of your home.

11. We will suggest ways to prepare your home for marketing.

12. We maintain continuous contact with financing sources.

13. We have the ability to follow up on prospects without making the seller appear overanxious.

14. We have the skill to diplomatically resolve personality conflicts that may arise.

15. We provide feedback of customers' reactions to your property — information they normally find difficult to communicate.

16. We are skilled in negotiating when we get down to price, terms, and conditions.

17. We provide a trustee account for escrow funds.

18. We provide smooth followthrough on obtaining the mortgage, signing the contracts, arranging termite and building inspection, and handling closing details.

19. We give friendly assistance to seller and buyer on the move.

20. We educate buyers on schools and government, recreation, and cultural facilities.

Professional Marketing Of Your Home Calls For:

1. Suggestions on ways to make it more saleable.

2. Market-comparable approach to pricing.

3. Calling our qualified customers.

4. Arranging appointments to show.

5. Advertising.

6. Apprising you of any change in market conditions.

7. Control of the customer while showing.

8. Educating customers on Wilton's values.

9. Following up on prospects for reactions, overcoming objections. Reporting back to you.

10. Submitting all offers promptly. All offers must be in writing and accompanied by a good faith deposit check.

11. Negotiating price, terms, and conditions.

12. Advising you how to counteroffer.

13. Obtaining the required financing.

14. Following through on deposits, escrow, contracts, inspections, settlement procedures, closing.

15. Treating all parties to the transaction with fairness and integrity.

Did You Know . . . ?

- *Rarely* does a prospect buy the house he or she answered the ad on. (Think back to the price on the ad that interested you when you were house-hunting. Wasn't it less than you eventually paid?) The buyer for your home may come to us on an ad for a lower-priced one; he or she needs educating on property values in our area by a trained salesperson.

- Buyers are vitally interested in what our area has to offer and *expect a tour of the town* and all the vital statistics. (Will you have the right answers for their many questions?)

- House buyers are *comparison shoppers.* (You have only one house to show them.)

- Most buyers are *too polite* to tell an owner what they don't like. (Our salespeople are skillful in drawing out the negatives so that they can be overcome.)

- Insincere and underqualified buyers avoid Realtors®. (We will not waste our time or yours with "lookers", and we're adept at interviewing.)

- When *mortgage funds are scarce,* our fine relationship of 25 years with lenders stands us in good stead. (Are you up to date on financing sources? Terms? VRM's, MID's, bridge or swing loans, etc.?) Are you aware of tax laws that apply to you?

- It is hard for owners to be *objective* in negotiating the price, terms, and conditions on the sale of their own home.

- Most property buyers in our area are *transferred executives* with a tight time schedule who expect professional service. They want to be shown the community and learn how it compares with other towns in terms of schools, tax structure, amenities, etc. They want to see only those properties that meet their specifications. They like to be personally referred to a choice of financing sources, and they want follow-up services performed promptly and efficiently. They rely on a recommended Realtor®.

Checklist For Organizing A Family Move

Date Done

1. If it's a company transfer, find out what the firm does and does not provide.
2. For dual-career families, ascertain job opportunities in new location.
3. Share news with children; show pictures of new area; emphasize benefits.
4. Go through present house and move all items that can be discarded to garage. Have a tag sale or donate these.
5. Make an inventory of all possessions to be moved, noting date and price of purchase. Carry this with you.

60 Days Before Move

6. List property with a Realtor®. Ask for suggestions regarding improvements.
7. Fix obvious defects (sagging gutter, loose doorknob, broken light switch, wobbly bannister, etc.).
8. Call moving company to get estimate; reserve date.
9. Obtain "change of address kit" from post office; notify magazines, credit card companies, others.
10. Begin to use up canned and frozen foods on hand.

30 Days Before Move

11. Obtain school, medical, dental records for family; carry with you.
12. Set up bank account in new area.
13. Call your insurance agent to find out if extra coverage should be carried on possessions in transit. Ask what coverage is provided if present house will be vacant.
14. Arrange travel plans; make reservations.
15. Check keys you'll give new owner; make a list of service persons you've used to leave in house.

7 Days Before Move

16. Arrange to give away what can't be moved: goldfish, gerbils, houseplants?
17. Pack to carry with you all important documents: birth certificates, eyeglass and other prescriptions, passports, etc.

Date Done

18. Return library books and any items "borrowed". Pick up anything being repaired or dry cleaned.
19. Call utility companies about date of transfer.
20. Arrange to have the house cleaned after you leave. If house will be vacant, arrange for maintenance.

FINALLY, pack a "fun and snax" bag if you're travelling with children.

. . . *To a Prospect You Haven't Met*

MAIN STREET • HOMETOWN, PT 00000 • 111-111-1111

Date

Name
Address

Dear _____:

    Thank you for calling on our ad for the "Solar Oriented Contemporary" house. I'm glad you're thinking of moving to our area, and we have several properties in the size, style, and price range you indicated.

    We have excellent brokers available in neighboring areas, and have asked them to send you information about other properties that may interest you.

    When we know your date of arrival, I'll schedule appointments so that you can cover the area conveniently. Because we can provide door-to-door service from your motel to inspect properties, you won't need to rent a car for house hunting.

    Some information about our area schools and our cultural and recreational facilities is enclosed.

    I'm looking forward to seeing you soon.

                    Sincerely yours,

                    _____

                         (signature)

Enclosures

. . . To a Prospect You've Taken Out

REALTOR

MAIN STREET • HOMETOWN, PT 00000 • 111-111-1111

```
                                      Date

     Name
     Address

     Dear _____

          It was a pleasure to show you properties yesterday.  I realize
     we don't have the house that you want right now.  You gave me a lot
     of good clues and guide lines, and I'll call you as soon as a listing
     is available that is "right" for you.

          Because you're a tennis buff, I'm enclosing information about our
     tennis clubs.

                         Sincerely yours,


                         _____
                              (signature)


     Enclosures
```

Note: **Substitute whatever material would be of interest to the prospect. For example, if one of the children is keen on swimming, send a "Y" brochure. If another child likes horses, send a "Riding Trail Guide". If the executive parent must travel a lot, send data on the airport limousine service and private driver services available. Tailor the last paragraph to the prospect!**

193

. . . To a "For Sale by Owner"

Anne Andrews
& Associates

MAIN STREET • HOMETOWN, PT 00000 • 111-111-1111

Date

Name
Address

Dear _____,

       Thank you for showing us your property today. We understand
you wish to try to market the house yourself, by advertising and personal
showings, in the hope of "saving a commission". But buyers may "discount"
the asking price because "there's no broker", and you may become
discouraged.

       We have marketing skills that may achieve better results. Our
office is open 7 days a week, and we would like to work for you to sell
the property. Our phone is answered around the clock. We screen prospects
to eliminate "lookers" and also those who are not qualified financially
for a house in your price range. We schedule appointments for showing,
and you need not be at home. By showing other houses, we are able to
educate buyers on fair market values here. With a "Tour of the Town",
we're able to interest a prospect in living here, and can answer their
questions on schools, zoning, government, the building code, sanitation,
taxes, and recreational and cultural amenities. While this is time consuming,
we must often "sell the town" before we can sell the house.

       We're skillful negotiators when an offer is submitted, trying to
obtain for you the best agreement with regard to price, terms, occupancy,
etc. We follow through on contract signing, contingencies, financing,
closing. We maintain a Trustee Account for escrow funds.

       As we've been Realtors since 1956, our banking contacts are
excellent, and we rarely have difficulty obtaining a mortgage for our
qualified buyers.

       If you decide to list with us, we'll prepare a Market Comparable
Data analysis on your house to assist you in determining your listing price.
It includes recent sales prices of similar houses and a listing of houses
that are currently competing with yours for the buyer's dollars.

       We will, of course, advertise your property and — more important —
be on the phone at once contacting prospects we have already qualified who
would seriously consider your house.

       I'll keep in touch, and do call me if you have any questions
about our marketing program for your property.

                      Sincerely yours,

                  _(signature)_____

. . . *To an Owner Who Has Asked Several Brokers to "Price" the House*

 *Anne Andrews & Associates*

MAIN STREET • HOMETOWN, PT 00000 • 111-111-1111

                                                    Date

Name
Address

Dear _____ ,

    Thank you for calling us about marketing your house, which I
enjoyed seeing today. You asked me to name a selling price, and I
told you it would be unprofessional to give an estimate of value without
researching market comparables. Our approach to estimating fair market
value is to have the property inspected by several brokers from our
office and then do independent research, before we put our heads together
to advise a listing price.

    As the other Realtors suggested, we recommend Multiple Listing
for maximum exposure of your house to prospects.

    If we are your listing broker, we will hold an open house, of
course, and advertise the property in the area media. Our associates are
well skilled in the arts of showing property, overcoming objections,
negotiating, obtaining a mortgage, and following through on all details.

    Please call us if you have any questions.

                                    Sincerely yours,

                                    _____
                                    (signature)

Note: **You may want to enclose a market comparable data analysis
and suggest a price range.**

195

MAIN STREET • HOMETOWN, PT 00000 • 111-111-1111

Date

Name
Address

Dear Mr. and Mrs. _____,

   We appreciate the opportunity to list and market your property,
and we will make every effort to achieve a satisfying property transaction.

   Our ads appear regularly in the area media that we have found most
productive, but you may not always see your house there. We have learned
that buyers usually answer ads for lesser priced properties and need
educating on market values as they gradually raise their sights.

   Do not be discouraged by occasional lulls in activity. There's an
ebb and flow, influenced by market conditions, weather, availability of
comparable properties, financing and holidays. We're on the job 24 hours
a day, 7 days a week, and will utilize every opportunity to show your
property to qualified prospects.

   All showings will be by appointment, but occasionally a broker may arrive
at your door unexpectedly. You have a right to refuse entry, but the
salesperson may have tried to reach you, or was able to upgrade the prospect
while showing lower-priced properties out on the road, and may have an
excellent would-be buyer in tow.

   The possibilities of a sale are greatly enhanced by the exterior and
interior appearances. A prospect may decline to see the inside of a house
when the outside is not appealing. An unkempt lawn, untrimmed shrubs, or
an unshovelled path in snow season will turn the potential buyer off.
So do minor defects, such as a loose doorknob, a cracked window pane, a wet
basement, or cracks in a ceiling.

   Real estate agents have skill and experience in answering objections
from the buyer. They welcome having the buyer express negatives so that
these can be overcome. If you are around, most buyers are silent, too
polite to voice objections. Therefore, we recommend you take a low profile
during showings. Take a walk or remain out of hearing. It's important
that the possible buyer talk freely.

It also helps to remove or confine any pets. Other distractions are
the TV or stereo. Turn on lights in dark halls or rooms where necessary
to create a warm feeling.

Consider a Tag Sale for all those items that you don't want to move
that are now squeezed into closets, piled up on the basement stairs, or
in the garage, or call Good Will or the Salvation Army. Your objective
is to display ample closet and storage space.

We are partners in getting your house sold. We've been in business
since 1956 and we want to share what we've learned with you.

Sincerely yours,

_____
(signature)

Note: **This letter must be revised according to the condition of the
property. Omit the sentences that are not appropriate.**

. . . *To Neighbors About Your New Listing*

MAIN STREET • HOMETOWN, PT 00000 • 111-111-1111

Date

Name
Address

Dear _____ ,

    We have just listed property at _____(address of listing)_____ .
As you know, this is an attractive home in a desirable neighborhood.

    Perhaps you know someone who would be interested in this house.
It has a living room with fireplace, a dining room, a well-equipped
kitchen, three bedrooms, and two baths. There's a delightful brick
patio.

    Please call us if you have any suggestions or questions.

                        Sincerely yours,

                        _____(signature)_____

Note: **Always obtain the owners' permission to send out this letter.
They may prefer that no neighbors know that the property is on
the market.**

198

. . . To a Client with Ad

 **Anne Andrews & Associates**

MAIN STREET • HOMETOWN, PT 00000 • 111-111-1111

Date

Name
Address

Dear _____ ,

    I thought you might like to see a copy of the ad on your house
that we ran in the Sunday paper.

Paste in a copy of the ad.

    We hope it will attract some qualified prospects we can show your
house to.

                Sincerely yours,

                _____
                     (signature)

. . . *To the Referring Broker*

Anne Andrews & Associates

MAIN STREET • HOMETOWN, PT 00000 • 111-111-1111

REFERRAL AGREEMENT

Date: _____

TO: _____

_____

_____

_____

Confirming our telephone conversation, the prospect we are referring is:

NAME: _____ HOME ADDRESS: _____

BUSINESS ADDRESS: _____

HOME PHONE: _____ BUSINESS PHONE: _____

REMARKS:

This referral will be on the basis of _____% to you as the selling or
renting broker and _____% to us as the referring broker after the listing
fee is paid. A prospect will be considered our referral if he or she buys
a house from you within two years from the date hereof. In the case of
rentals, we shall be recognized if the prospect purchases within one year
of lease expiration.

We would appreciate your acknowledging this referral by signing and
returning the enclosed copy to us. Thank you.

ACCEPTED:

_____

_____

_____   Very truly yours,

_____

... *To the Referring Broker with Check*

Anne Andrews
& Associates

Name   Date
Address

Dear _____ ,

It is a pleasure to send you this check for the referral prospect
we sold. The breakdown is:

Sales Price   _____

Gross Commission   _____

Less: Listing Broker Fee   _____

Office Net Commission   _____

Referral   _____

We look forward to selling more for you.

Cordially,

MAIN STREET • HOMETOWN, PT 00000 • 111-111-1111

Date

Name
Address

Dear _____,

    We have just sold the home of _____(names)_____, at
_____(location)_____. Your new neighbors, ____(names)____,
will be moving in next month.

    The _____(purchasers)_____ are from ____(city)_____
and have two children, Tom, age 6, and Betsey, age 3. They look forward
to being residents of _____(your town)_____.

    The property generated a good deal of interest. If you know of
anyone in the area who is thinking of selling, we now have some qualified
prospective buyers who like the neighborhood. Do give us a call.

                Sincerely yours,

                _____(signature)_____

Note: Always obtain the permission of the purchasers before sending this letter.

. . . *To a Buyer on the Monthly Cost of Home Ownership*

MAIN STREET • HOMETOWN, PT 00000 • 111-111-1111

```
MONTHLY COST OF HOME OWNERSHIP prepared

For: ...................................     By: ....................

Purchase price of property                        ....................
Less cash equity                                  ....................
Mortgage of _____@_____%          ....................


Monthly debt service                              ....................
Monthly real estate taxes                         ....................
Monthly insurance                                 ....................
Total Monthly expenses                            ....................


Deductible items:
    Monthly interest (average) ............
    Monthly taxes              ............

Total deductible for taxpayer using itemized deductions   ....................
Tax bracket _____% x total deductions = ......... tax savings


Total monthly                                     ....................
Less tax savings                                  ....................
Net cost                                          ....................


Less monthly equity build-up (averaged)           ....................
Net Cost                                          ....................
Less monthly appreciation estimated at 10%
per annum ÷ 12 =                                  ....................


REAL MONTHLY COST OF HOME OWNERSHIP               ....................
```

Transaction Record

TRANSACTION RECORD

SELLER: BUYER:

ADDRESS: ADDRESS:

PHONE: PHONE:

PROPERTY: _____   PRICE: _____

FINANCING:

CONTINGENCIES:

TO BE INCLUDED:
    Range
    Dishwasher
    TV antennae
    Carpeting
    Other:

ATTORNEY FOR SELLER: ATTORNEY FOR BUYER:

BINDER SIGNED: BINDER CHECK DEPOSITED:

CONTRACT SIGNED: CLOSING DATE:

UTILITIES:
    CL&P
    Telephone
    Oil
    Other:

SOURCE OF PROSPECT: LISTING BROKER:

                                           SELLING BROKER:

Ledger Sheets — Cash Receipts and Cash Disbursements

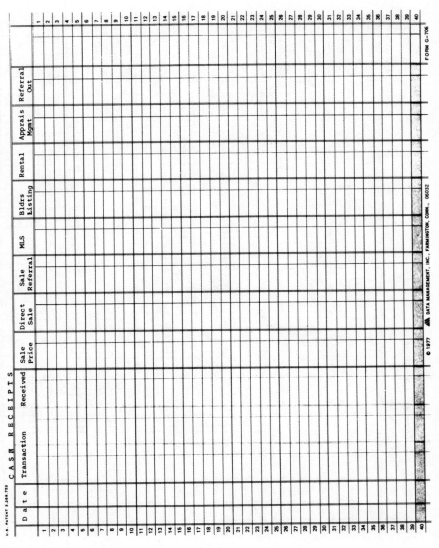

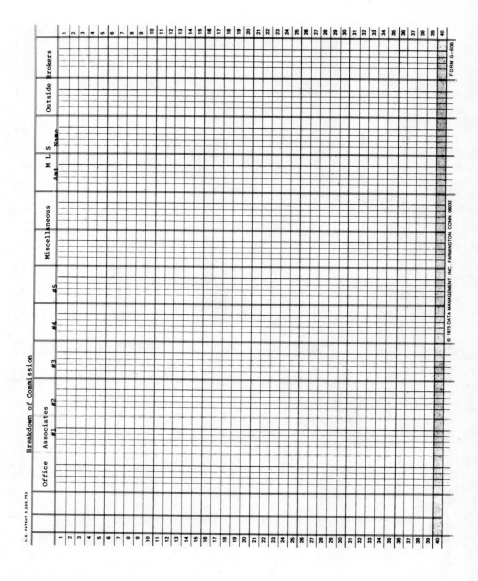

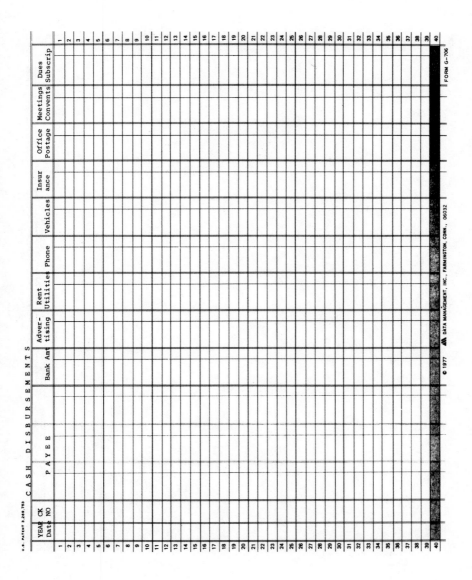

CASH DISBURSEMENTS

YEAR Date	CK NO	P A Y E E	Bank Amt	Adver-tising	Rent Utilities	Phone	Vehicles	Insur ance	Office Postage	Meetings Convents	Dues Subscrip
1											
2											
3											
4											
5											
6											
7											
8											
9											
10											
11											
12											
13											
14											
15											
16											
17											
18											
19											
20											
21											
22											
23											
24											
25											
26											
27											
28											
29											
30											
31											
32											
33											
34											
35											
36											
37											
38											
39											
40											

U.S. PATENT 3,260,783

© 1977 ▲▲ DATA MANAGEMENT, INC., FARMINGTON, CONN., 06032

FORM G-706

Repairs Maint	Customer Gifts	Promo tion	Salaries	Taxes	Commiss ions	Legal & Accting			Equipmt	Miscellaneous	
1											1
2											2
3											3
4											4
5											5
6											6
7											7
8											8
9											9
10											10
11											11
12											12
13											13
14											14
15											15
16											16
17											17
18											18
19											19
20											20
21											21
22											22
23											23
24											24
25											25
26											26
27											27
28											28
29											29
30											30
31											31
32											32
33											33
34											34
35											35
36											36
37											37
38											38
39											39
40											40

Writing an Appraisal Report

Tailor your presentation style of the appraisal to the client who requested it. It may be a bank or corporation that furnishes its own forms for the appraiser to fill out. You may wish to submit the report in an attractive folder and use color photographs instead of black and white. Both front and rear views of a house are helpful. It is wise to agree in advance on what your fee will be, although there may be a range, depending on the amount of time involved in research and preparation. You may wish to include your qualifications as an appraiser, especially if the appraisal will be used in court as part of a foreclosure action, a divorce agreement, or an estate being probated. You may be subpoenaed to appear in court to substantiate the appraisal report so keep all your work notes. If you are required to appear in court, you are entitled to be paid for your time.

Send your report with a covering letter and the bill for services rendered.

Sample Covering Letter

MAIN STREET • HOMETOWN, PT 00000 • 111-111-1111

                                                    Date

Name
Address

Dear _____,

    Enclosed is the appraisal report you requested, and a statement for
our services. I've been a Realtor since 1960, and appraising is a
continuing activity of mine.

    I trust you will find the report helpful in making your decision
about whether or not you wish to sell the property at this time.

                          Sincerely yours,

                          _____
                                (signature)

Enclosures

Sample Narrative Appraisal Report

Re: 246 Robin Lane
    Hometown, CT 06483

The above property was inspected February 16, 19XX, to determine fair
market value if the property is sold in 30 to 90 days.

Robin Lane is a dead-end street in a residential neighborhood. It is
zoned for single family houses on plots that are a minimum of one acre in
size. Most of the houses were built 10 to 15 years ago and are well maintained.
The subject property is 12 years old and located on 1.1 acres. A location
survey is on file, #7431. The land is fairly open, with large front and back
yards.

The exterior siding is wood shingles, set about 12" to the weather, recently
stained a dark brown. The trim was painted white a year ago. The exterior
is in good condition. The foundation planting is kept trimmed. Sliding
glass doors open from the living room onto a 12' x 16' flagstone patio. The
one-car garage is attached.

The interior has an entry hall, a living room with wood-burning fireplace,
a dining room, a kitchen, 3 bedrooms, and 1-1/2 baths. The interior living
area is approximately 1600 square feet. The interior is well maintained.
There are wooden floors in all rooms except the kitchen, bathroom, and lavatory,
where there is vinyl flooring installed 2 years ago. An unfinished attic is
reached by pull-down stairs. The attic and side walls have 3" to 4" of
fiberglass insulation.

Baseboard hot water heating is supplied by the original oil burner. All
windows have storm and screen sash; there are no storm doors at the front
and rear entrances. Hot water is supplied by the furnace. There is city water
and sewage lines.

There is a partial basement with room for a work bench as well as laundry
equipment and the furnace. Appliances that are included in the sale are the
electric range, dishwasher, washing machine, and dryer.

The assessed value of the property on the 1980 Grand List was $55,000.
At the current mill rate of 30 mills, the 1981 taxes are $1650.00.

The highest and best use of the property is residential. Schools and
shopping are 6 to 8 blocks away.

Recent Sales of Market Comparables

	Address	Description	Date of Sale	Price
1.	46 Highfield Road	3 bdrm, 1 bath ranch built 1971	12/1/XX	$76,000
2.	314 Graham Lane	3 bdrm, 2 bath ranch built 1969 (has screened porch)	1/15/XX	$79,500
3.	29 Ledgebrook Road	3 bdrm, 1-1/2 bath ranch built 1968	1/30/XX	$77,500

Based on the Market Comparable Approach, my estimate of Fair Market Value is
$78,000. We are coming into the spring market, mortgages are available, and
real estate activity is picking up.

_____ (signature) _____

Outline for Residential Appraisal

1. The purpose of this appraisal is:

   To determine Fair Market Value of a home to be sold in the next 30-90 days.

2. Location of property:

3. Date property was inspected:

4. Description of the neighborhood:

5. Description of the property:

   a) Land -

   b) Building exterior -

   c) Landscaping -

   d) Building interior -

   e) Utilities and improvements -

   f) Heat, hot water -

   g) Garage, any other structures -

   h) Basement, attic -

   i) Included as part of the premises -

6. Assessed value, mill rate, taxes:

7. Highest and best use of the property:

8. Recent sales of market comparables:

Address	Description	Date of Sale	Sale Price
a.			
b.			
c.			

9. Estimate of value by market comparable approach:

10. General remarks:

    (Optional: Attach a photograph of the property)

    _____ (Signature) _____

Note: **Prepare a market data comparable form and keep it in your file.**

Market Data Comparable Form

BASIC PROPERTY DATA	STYLE	SQ FEET	RMS	BED RMS	DEN	BATHS	GAR	AGE	LOT SIZE	Special Terms &/or Features	DAYS ON MKT	LISTING PRICE	CURRENT SALE OR LIST PRICE
SUBJECT ADDRESS													

COMPETITIVE PROPERTIES FOR SALE NOW

ESTIMATE AVG. VALUE

RECENTLY SOLD PROPERTIES

APPROX. INDICATED VALUE

EXPIRED/OFF MARKET PAST ___ MONTHS

APPROX. INDICATED VALUE (Less Than)

ADDITIONAL INFORMATION RELATED TO SUBJECT PROPERTY

BUYER APPEAL

1. Location
2.
3.
4.
Market Demand

DRAWBACKS

1.
2.
3.
4.
Economic Conditions

INDICATED PRICE RANGE

Top Competitive Market Value
Lowest Competitive Market Value
Probable Final Sales Price
Suggested Starting

LS Form I Conn. Assoc. of Realtors

213

Recommended Reading

J. D. Batten, *Tough Minded Management* (New York: American Management Association, 1969).

Walter B. Bayless, Jr., *You Can Win the Real Estate Game* (Reston, Va.: Reston Publishing Co., 1979).

Samuel Eilon, *Aspects of Management* (Elmsford, N.Y.: Pergamon Press, 1977).

Encyclopedia of Real Estate Appraising (Englewood Cliffs, N.J.: Prentice-Hall, 1980).

Julius Fast, *Body Language* (New York: Simon & Schuster, 1971).

Henry S. Harrison, REALTOR®, MAI, *Houses: The Illustrated Guide to Construction, Design and Systems* (Chicago: Realtors National Marketing Institute®, 1974).

Napoleon Hill, *Think and Grow Rich* (Greenwich, Conn.: Fawcett Publications, 1937).

C. R. Jacobus and D. R. Levi, *Real Estate Law* (Reston, Va.: Reston Publishing Co., 1980).

Charlotte Korn, *A Real Estate Agent's Guide to Successful Sales and Listings* (Reston, Va.: Reston Publishing Co., 1976).

Douglas McGregor, *The Professional Manager* (New York: McGraw-Hill, 1967).

R. Alec Mackenzie, *The Time Trap: Managing Your Way Out* (New York: Amacom, 1972).

Maxwell Maltz, M.D., F.I.C.S., *Psycho-Cybernetics* (New York: Prentice-Hall, 1960).

Bruce Marcus, *Marketing Professional Services in Real Estate* (Chicago: Realtors National Marketing Institute®, 1981).

Albert J. Mayer III, *Readings in Management for the Real Estate Executive* (Chicago: Realtors National Marketing Institute®, 1978).

Realtors National Marketing Institute®, *Real Estate Office Management, People Functions Systems* (Chicago: the Institute, 1975).

Theodor Reik, *Listening with the Third Ear* (New York: Grove Press, 1971).

Kirkpatrick Sale, *Human Scale* (New York: Coward, McCann & Geoghegan, 1980).

John R. Taylor, *How To Start and Succeed in a Business of Your Own* (Reston, Va.: Reston Publishing Co., 1978).

Leon Tec, M.D., *Targets — How To Set Goals for Yourself and Reach Them!* (New York: Harper & Row, 1980).

Index